YOUR PROPHETIC LIFE MAP

YOUR
PROPHETIC
LIFE MAP

YOUR PROPHETIC LIFE MAP

A GUIDE TO A GOD-CRAFTED LIFE

Steve Witt

EMANATE
BOOKS

Published in Nashville, Tennessee, by Emanate Books, an imprint of Thomas Nelson. Emanate Books and Thomas Nelson are registered trademarks of HarperCollins Christian Publishing, Inc.

Thomas Nelson titles may be purchased in bulk for educational, business, fund-raising, or sales promotional use. For information, please e-mail SpecialMarkets@ThomasNelson.com.

Unless otherwise noted, Scripture quotations are taken from the New King James Version®. © 1982 by Thomas Nelson. Used by permission. All rights reserved.

Scripture quotations marked ESV are from the ESV® Bible (The Holy Bible, English Standard Version®). Copyright © 2001 by Crossway, a publishing ministry of Good News Publishers. Used by permission. All rights reserved.

Scripture quotations marked GW are from God's Word®. Copyright © 1995 God's Word to the Nations. Used by permission of Baker Publishing Group. All rights reserved.

Scripture quotations marked THE MESSAGE are from The Message. Copyright © by Eugene H. Peterson 1993, 1994, 1995, 1996, 2000, 2001, 2002. Used by permission of NavPress. All rights reserved. Represented by Tyndale House Publishers, Inc.

Scripture quotations marked NIV are from the Holy Bible, New International Version®, NIV®. Copyright © 1973, 1978, 1984, 2011 by Biblica, Inc.® Used by permission of Zondervan. All rights reserved worldwide. www.Zondervan.com. The "NIV" and "New International Version" are trademarks registered in the United States Patent and Trademark Office by Biblica, Inc.®

Scripture quotations marked NLT are from the Holy Bible, New Living Translation. © 1996, 2004, 2007, 2013, 2015 by Tyndale House Foundation. Used by permission of Tyndale House Publishers, Inc., Carol Stream, Illinois 60188. All rights reserved.

Scripture quotations marked TPT are from The Passion Translation®. Copyright © 2017 by BroadStreet Publishing® Group, LLC. Used by permission. All rights reserved. thePassionTranslation.com.

Any Internet addresses, phone numbers, or company or product information printed in this book are offered as a resource and are not intended in any way to be or to imply an endorsement by Thomas Nelson, nor does Thomas Nelson vouch for the existence, content, or services of these sites, phone numbers, companies, or products beyond the life of this book.

ISBN 978-0-7852-2454-9 (TP)
ISBN 978-0-7852-2455-6 (eBook)

Library of Congress Control Number:2019943786

Printed in the United States of America

19 20 21 22 23 LSC 10 9 8 7 6 5 4 3 2 1

I wrote this book with several extraordinary people in mind:
my children Megan, Lauren, Ashley, Joshua, and spouses

Also to an emerging generation of amazing grandchildren:
Moses, Josephine, Maxwell, Madeline, and the others to come!
Set the world on fire!

To my Canadian wife of more than 40 years: Cindy
You've lived this in fullness.

CONTENTS

CONTENTS

FOREWORD

Your Prophetic Life Map is an extremely timely book for the people of God. Most of us struggle with understanding our role in seeing the fulfillment of the promises of God for our lives. Some wait and do nothing, stating that their job is to *stand by and see the salvation of the Lord which He will accomplish for you today.* This is a very legitimate posture for the believer to take as it's in the Bible. And yet others will state, *the kingdom of heaven suffers violence, and the violent take it by force.* That group will point to the fact that faith needs an action, and sometimes that action involves spiritual warfare. This is also a legitimate position to take, as Jesus taught His disciples about this in Mark 10. Confusion over our role is what often sours the journey of the average believer.

I believe that what God has given my friend and author, Steve Witt, will help add clarity to this vital subject, as we are on a relational journey. I prefer the outcome where promises, destinies, and impact on the world around us become more fully realized. But Jesus likes the journey whereby we become a people who can live in the glory for which we were created.

If fulfilled promises were all that this book brought into our lives, it would be worth its weight in gold. But the author goes far beyond the subject of fulfillment, making this book priceless. Most of us pour our lives out for the Lord that we might see the great impact of our devotion to Christ. We desire His power flowing through us in a way that confronts the impossible, bringing it under influence of the One who knows no impossibilities. Simply put, many of us are focused on the outcome. And while *Your Prophetic Life Map* satisfies that need, its primary focus is profound in that it is focused on the journey and not just the destination. In the journey, Jesus put His attention on what we are becoming.

I have felt for many years that the measure of the will of God we get to enjoy in this life is often determined by our maturity. Picture it this way: the will of God is glorious and wonderful (*on earth as it is in heaven*). But it is also weighty, carrying with it greater and greater responsibilities. The character of many in history couldn't carry the weight involved in the level of miracles surrounding their lives. There were cracks in their foundations that were almost unnoticeable when little was happening. But those character flaws became all too obvious under the weight of the greater glory. And yet we know that God's intent is that the reality of His world would influence and shape this one.

Here is the beauty of what this author does for each of us. He draws us into the book because of our God-given hunger for fulfillment. But then he works to build in us a substantial foundation that will hold under the increasing weight of what God intends to do in and through our lives. Remember, transformed people transform nations. This is His heart. To have a people who represent Jesus well in purity and power. It is this group who will help to fulfill the mandate to disciple nations. The bottom line is that this book helps us to be joyfully engaged in the process, not just the outcome.

One of the things that makes this book so rich is that it was born out of a life lived in absolute surrender to Jesus. Because of this, you won't find theories and religious rhetoric that are used to fill the weak places in so many books. These insights were given to one of the most trusted men I know—Steve Witt. He has been a personal strength and inspiration to me for many years. The lessons learned in a war are not soon forgotten. That is the reality of this book.

Your Prophetic Life Map is very practical, inspirational, and prophetic. My prayer is that the word of the Lord that has been spoken over your life would come to the surface while reading this book. May these words prompt you to ask the challenging questions about the direction and purpose of your life. And, in the process, may extraordinary courage be your portion to see everything come to pass that God has spoken.

Bill Johnson
Bethel Church, Redding, CA
Author of *The Way of Life* and *Raising Giant-Killers*

INTRODUCTION

I f you've ever tried to learn a foreign language, then you know the process requires more than just memorizing vocabulary and parroting speech. Fluency in a new language requires an understanding of the culture from those who regularly speak it. You need to keep in mind certain customs, quirks, and habits. You have to glimpse the beauty, mystery, and music of the culture in order to speak the language and understand its cadence, rhythm, and tempo.

This book is about learning a new language. In these pages, we will explore what's usually called prophetic faith. Followers of Jesus who speak about the prophetic are typically referring to a personal experience in which they encounter and attempt to understand messages from God. The word *prophecy* comes from the Greek and literally means "a discourse emanating from divine inspiration and declaring the purpose of God." In other words, it's communication from God to you conveying direction or clarification about your life or future events.

This practice makes some people uncomfortable. Many of them don't fully understand or trust the meaning of what's called prophetic in the church. This has created a fear of hearing, understanding, and responding to the voice of God. While, admittedly, many squirrelly things can happen in the name of hearing from God, it doesn't mean we can't talk to Him and hear from Him.

After all, that's what prayer is all about—a conversation with the Lord. If we're not talking to God and listening to Him, it makes it hard to know all that He wants us to know. It makes it even tougher to live by faith. Consider how frustrating it would be to communicate with someone if you weren't willing to at least try to speak their language—especially if they were trying to give you directions to your destination!

From the beginning our Creator's desire was to know us as His children and be known. When Adam and Eve freely chose to disobey God, their rebellion created a separation that was restored in the person of Jesus Christ. He opened the gateway of understanding and clarity. The Bible says that "the testimony of Jesus . . . is the Spirit of prophecy" (Rev. 19:10 NIV). All the things you need to know about God are revealed in your relationship with Jesus.

And Jesus wants us to understand. His parables were crafted for the hungry and discerning. Nonetheless, His disciples often struggled to grasp what Jesus was really talking about. It took intention, reflection, and discernment to learn the language of heaven.

For us today, it also requires the Holy Spirit's guidance. On the day of Pentecost, when the Spirit descended and ignited God's presence in His followers, how we can know and communicate with God forever changed. Peter described this fiery explosion of God's power descending as the fulfillment of the ancient prophecy we find in Joel 2. The gift of the Spirit provides us with an anointing of revelation, an awareness of heaven on earth. At Pentecost, it was as if heaven had been punctured so that spiritual gifts suddenly poured out on those seeking God.

Peter said this promise they had received was intended for them, their children, and all who were "afar off" (Acts 2:39 NIV). Consequently, we know today that Holy Spirit–led people are still prophetic. Scripture explains that through the Holy Spirit, God will show you the future, reveal secrets, and unveil your purpose. From this impartment, God will also give you new life, victory, purification, and encouragement. Your prophetic gift will reveal things that bring amazement, provoke criticism, and facilitate transformation.

These were certainly the results in the early church, where prophecy ranked as a high priority among believers. In his letter to the Corinthians, Paul explained how prophecy is a gift of the Holy Spirit that allows us to speak to others for "their strengthening, encouraging, and comfort" (1 Cor. 14:3 NIV). He went on to stress, "I would like every one of you to speak in tongues, *but I would rather have you prophesy*" (v. 5 NIV, my emphasis).

If the prophetic is a journey of discovering what God thinks and says about you, then the Bible is your compass. Scripture provides direction and orientation for understanding what it means to know God and the history of His people. In God's Word, we encounter the gift of His Son, Jesus, who was born a baby, lived as a man, and died as a sacrifice for our sins, only to rise again as our Savior. After revealing Himself to His followers as the risen Christ, Jesus ascended to heaven and sent the gift of the Holy Spirit to us.

Throughout my life I have experienced the power of a relationship with the Holy Spirit. I'm convinced God shares His Spirit as our guide on the adventure of faith to which we're all invited. I have noticed over my years of experiencing the prophetic heart of God that more truth is realized in the deepest, most intimate places of our relationship with Him. As you pursue a closer relationship with God, you are privy to His prophetic wisdom.

You see, your proximity matters, and it determines your ability to understand His communication. It's easy to hear someone shout across a crowded room, but if you want to hear the intimate secrets of a confidant, then you must come much closer to hear Him whisper. Jesus ministered to the multitudes, and they experienced a certain awareness of His love. The disciples who followed Christ experienced a more meaningful awareness due to their closeness with Him. Three of these disciples—Peter, James, and John—experienced even more of this intense closeness. Ultimately, John, the disciple who leaned on Jesus at the Last Supper, received the greatest revelation, which we know as Revelation, the last book of the Bible.

When you lean on Jesus, expect to be amazed at what will happen!

Your pursuit of Jesus will unveil the unknown and produce greater wisdom. The Holy Spirit will reveal Christ's presence in cathedrals and crawl spaces, forests and factories, schools and skate parks, kitchens and cubicles, in the brightest sunrise and the darkest night. The closer you grow in love with the Lord, the more you begin to know what He would do in any situation. It's no different from a son or daughter coming to understand how their parents make decisions and discern directions. The wisdom of God allows those who are prophetic to mature and move forward into His will for their lives.

You are invited on this path of understanding. In this book, I want to share what I've learned about hearing the voice of God and encountering His presence in the world around us. You will learn to speak this spiritual language of longing. You will also begin to see how God has moved in your past without you even knowing it. Your interpretation of your life as seen through His loving presence can now direct your tomorrows and reveal answers to questions like these you've been afraid to ask yourself:

Why am I here? What's my purpose in life? What story is my life telling? How is God revealing Himself and His character through the twists and turns of my faith journey? How do I position myself to move in the direction He has always been taking me?

Finding these answers requires solving the puzzle that displays your prophetic life map. This is the map you're called to follow, the puzzle you long to piece together. But you have to be willing to see the pieces of the puzzle clearly. Your life can have greater meaning when you pause and look at your wounds, mistakes, choices, gifts, triumphs, and trials through the eyes of the Holy Spirit. Then you can see the pattern being formed even from your life's most painful moments. You become prophetic, fluent in the language of heaven, able to hear God's voice and celebrate His gifts as you share them with others.

Jesus spoke this language because He Himself is the Word made flesh (John 1:14). As the ultimate translator of God's grace, He proclaimed, "I absolutely know who I am, where I've come from, and where I'm going" (John 8:14 TPT). The more you follow Him, the more fluent you become in knowing and living out your own identity, your purpose, and your destination.

There's nothing scary or crazy about this process. Knowing God is like discovering a treasure map. Being a prophetic person simply means loving Jesus so deeply that you become attuned to His presence within you. Like someone who knows what their beloved is thinking without saying a word, you become fluent in the language of His love, able to read the prophetic life map unfolding around you.

Every map has a legend in which symbols are identified, sites are indicated, distances are determined, and the scale is revealed. This book is your key to reading the treasure map that God has given you. If you love the Lord and want to know Him more intimately, it's time to read your map and take giant strides on your journey.

Ready to take the first step? Then turn the page.

CHAPTER 1

MAP MAKING

Partnering with God

Your kingdom come.
Your will be done
On earth as it is in heaven.
—LUKE 11:2

If God is your partner, make your plans BIG!
—D. L. MOODY

Partnering with God often leads us to unexpected destinations. Just ask astronaut Buzz Aldrin, the second man to walk on the moon. After he and Neil Armstrong landed in the Sea of Tranquility on July 20, 1969, Aldrin prepared to take communion on the moon. He had met with his pastor, Dean Woodruff, who had blessed the bread and wine accompanying Aldrin, along with a tiny silver chalice.

At the time, NASA resisted disclosing Aldrin's communion service due to an ongoing legal battle sparked by a reading from Genesis by the crew of Apollo 8 while orbiting the moon the previous year (1968). Consequently, a radio blackout permitted Aldrin time to take a step in new spiritual territory—literally. He later wrote of his experience:

> In the radio blackout I opened the little plastic packages which contained bread and wine. I poured the wine into the chalice our church had given me. In the one-sixth gravity of the moon the wine curled slowly and gracefully up the side of the cup. It was interesting to think that the very first liquid ever poured on the moon, and the first food eaten there, were communion elements.
>
> And so, just before I partook of the elements, I read the words which I had chosen to indicate our trust that as man probes into space we are in fact acting in Christ.
>
> I sensed especially strongly my unity with our church back home, and with the Church everywhere.
>
> I read: "I am the vine, you are the branches. Whoever remains in me, and I in him, will bear much fruit; for you can do nothing without me" (John 15:5 TEV).[1]

What a great example of boldly celebrating a divine partnership with God! The story remained under the radar but surfaced years later as a dynamic example of one person's out-of-this-world faith. Some have even called it the first "co*moon*ion"!

All joking aside, Buzz Aldrin strengthened his partnership with God even on the moon. While you and I may not venture into space, we can still experience our own unique, intimate relationship with the Creator of universes and galaxies. Because no matter where you may be in your life right now, you're on a spiritual journey.

You have a heavenly Father who has given you incredible gifts. He designed you to experience life to the fullest and created you to enjoy the satisfaction that only comes from living out your divine purpose.

Your mission is simple: discover your God-given design while growing closer to the Lord and deeper in your knowledge of Him. If you'll permit me to be your humble guide and fellow pilgrim, I'd love to help you find your way using your prophetic life map.

TRAVELING LIGHT

I want to help you find your destiny in and through Jesus Christ because He is the center of everything in life. Following your prophetic life map means knowing God and following the example of Jesus as you're guided by the Holy Spirit. While I can't provide specific, personalized directions for you, I can help you discover your map and inspire you to move forward on your pilgrimage of faith. As a fellow traveler, I've been pursuing these principles for decades, and my goal is to help you learn from your past while letting go of unnecessary baggage, live in the joy of the present moment, and venture toward the glorious future God has for you.

I don't have all the answers, but God has blessed me with a few glimmers of wisdom on my journey. I began my career on a dual track: as a church planter and a business instructor for an international training course. Surprisingly enough, I quickly discovered that my business training served me well in understanding biblical principles of God's kingdom. While the Bible is the first and foremost guide for what we're about to explore together, I will sometimes bring in other sources to help orient us on our spiritual journey. In fact, many of the examples and references included come from the business world as well as from history books.

My love for Saint Patrick and the influence of Irish Celtic culture also color my guidance in these pages. I became enamored with him years ago while reading *How the Irish Saved Civilization* by Thomas Cahill. In one generation, that fifth-century missionary won more than half a nation's population to Christ. No one is perfect, but the amazing story of how Patrick returned to his captors, pagans of the highest order, with the message of the gospel still resonates powerfully today. Amazing customs, art, and history arise from Celtic culture and frequently remind us of the power of Christ as the heart of our life's journey.

I have also created numerous charts to help guide you during this journey of discovery. They are sandwiched in at appropriate intervals with plenty of explanation. Please take time to look at them and meditate on them. This will help you not only absorb the material but make it your own.

While GPS and the use of online map apps have eclipsed our reliance on old, impossible-to-fold-the-same-way-twice paper maps, I hope you'll agree that there's something powerful and comforting about a battered Rand McNally or dog-eared Collins atlas that's seen you through dozens of vacations and road trips. The maps I love the most are marked up, worn out, and highlighted. Like my favorite books, they're the creased, flimsy maps with routes traced and destinations circled. Whether you're flipping pages or scrolling screens as you read this book, I pray this book will become your familiar friend, a trusted guide on your daily journey toward knowing God.

LADDERS AND BRIDGES

Discovering your prophetic life map is nothing new—just the opposite; it's as ancient as humanity's pursuit of knowing God. Better yet, it's as timely as the way God wants to speak to you personally at this very moment! Throughout the pages of the Bible, God repeatedly reveals His desire to partner with us, His children. Time and again, from Genesis to Revelation, it's clear that human actions on earth have correlating actions in heaven. Normal daily actions performed through the power of God for His kingdom can have heavenly consequences.

Consider that when asked by the disciples how to pray, Jesus provided the perfect model for divine communication. His example serves as a framework for how you and I can address God as our Father each day, asking that His "will be done on earth as it is in heaven" (Matt. 6:10 NIV). Our request unlocks heaven on earth. Our prayers are not just words but keys to unleash God's power over our world.

We may downplay the day-to-day framework we live in, but the spiritual reality is that we're all here on this earth, each and every one of us, for a heavenly purpose. Your relationships produce supernatural consequences, your job determines eternal consequences, and your daily choices reflect how you move through the landscape of divine possibility. That's why it's helpful to recognize the map God provides for you on this journey.

Attuned to his presence permeating our lives, we carry God with us into every scenario, whether on the moon or in the lions' den, the boardroom, the bullpen, or the belly of a whale. One of my favorite depictions of this reality emerges in the Old Testament from Jacob's dream:

> [Jacob] had a dream in which he saw a stairway resting on the earth, with its top reaching to heaven, and the angels of God were ascending and descending on it. There above it stood the LORD, and he said: "I am the LORD, the God of your father Abraham and the God of Isaac. I will give you and your descendants the land on which you are lying. Your descendants will be like the dust of the earth, and you will spread out to the west and to the east, to the north and to the south. All peoples on earth will be blessed through you and your offspring. I am with you and will watch over you wherever you go, and I will bring you back

to this land. I will not leave you until I have done what I have promised you."

When Jacob awoke from his sleep, he thought, "Surely the LORD is in this place, and I was not aware of it." (Gen. 28:12–16 NIV)

While running from his twin brother, Esau, whom he had tricked out of his birthright, Jacob took a break and grabbed some sleep. In his dream, where he saw a ladder extending from earth into the heavens, with angels continuously coming down and climbing back up again, note that the angelic activity originated in an *earthly realm*. With a ladder between the two realms, angels, God's messengers and agents of protection for us, travel back and forth. The ladder in Jacob's dream is basically a bridge, connecting the vertical with the horizontal. He realized, "Surely the LORD is in this place, and I was not aware of it" (v. 16 NIV). How often do we fail to recognize that God is also with us? Even when we're somewhere we know we shouldn't be or don't want to be, God is in that place with us.

We simply need to climb the ladder between earth and heaven.

KEYS TO THE KINGDOM

Thanks to the gift of God's Spirit, we don't have to climb that ladder based on our own efforts. In Christ we have a permanent ladder to bridge our lives on earth with God's power in heaven. When Jesus was establishing the framework of the emerging church, He spoke several truths reinforcing this connection. In Matthew 16 we see how Peter won his Master's identity quiz question: "Who do men say that I am?" Several of the disciples replied before Jesus gave them the zinger, "Who do *you* say I am?" (v. 15 NIV). Simon Peter, in his impetuous way, blurted out, "You are the Messiah, the Son of the living God"

(v. 16 NIV). Struck by the way His friend and follower recognized Him for who He is, Jesus observed that the only way Peter could have known this truth was through the Father.

Jesus then began to prophesy over His disciple, revealing that he is indeed "Peter," a name meaning "stone or rock," upon which Jesus would build his church. Although many interpretive views have come out over the years, my studies lead me to conclude that Jesus was most likely referring to the person of Peter as a founder. Jesus went on to declare that the church would begin with Peter, and the emerging framework would be powerful. The gates of hell would not prevail against such a fortress, and mighty keys to heaven would be given to him.

For us as followers of Christ today, there is still a connection between recognizing who Jesus is and discovering our own identities. Matthew, another of Jesus' disciples, described a church of called-out followers with immense heavenly authority on earth. Called by Jesus Himself, this group emerged as an apostolic class of leaders serving in what's often called the fivefold ministry of the church:

> So Christ himself gave the *apostles*, the *prophets*, the *evangelists*, the *pastors* and *teachers*, to equip his people for works of service, so that the body of Christ may be built up until we all reach unity in the faith and in the knowledge of the Son of God and become mature, attaining to the whole measure of the fullness of Christ. (Eph. 4:11–13 NIV, my emphasis)

This church has authority to invade hellish strongholds here on earth and also to bring solutions from heaven with the keys freely given by Jesus to equip His followers.

These keys unlock our sacred partnership with God. Our Father entrusts His favor upon us when we surrender our ways to Him in order to further His heavenly kingdom here on earth. In other words, keys to bind and loose from an earthly standpoint create a corresponding response from a heavenly realm. When you pray to God, He responds, and heaven recalibrates with a reciprocal response here on earth. When you bind evil activities from having power over you, heaven reflects God's power as if mirroring the victory Christ has already won over the Enemy. When you loose blessing, favor, health, and abundant life, the power of God's goodness is released in heaven toward earth.

FULL THROTTLE

In a conversation with His disciples about how to handle people who have sinned against us, Jesus also explained how we can experience this kind of power to express God's power here on earth:

> Assuredly, I say to you, whatever you bind on earth will be bound in heaven, and whatever you loose on earth will be loosed in heaven.
>
> Again I say to you that if two of you agree on earth concerning anything that they ask, it will be done for them by My Father in heaven. For where two or three are gathered together in My name, I am there in the midst of them. (Matt. 18:18–20)

Notice here again, your actions have heavenly consequences. The word translated into English here as "agree on" carries the connotation of a symphony or choir coming together to make a harmonious sound as one. When you create a symphony of agreement internally with God and externally with other people, then the power of heaven is released.

Again this agreement is "on earth." This reality reflects a believer's authority, given by Jesus, to colonize, or as I like to say "heavenize," our current temporal, mortal realm on earth with the eternal, immortal realities of heaven. You pray and bring heaven's solutions to a broken earth. When you agree with others for wanting the impossible, Jesus promises He will be in your midst.

Empowered by God, we have the ability to operate as His conduits here on earth. Often, the only thing stopping us is ourselves. Our doubt, disbelief, and fear often prevent us from opening our hearts full throttle. God is waiting for our action and is ready to distribute the results that are needed. We simply must embrace this collaborative partnership as we seek to love Him and know Him. Then the supernatural power of God's Spirit flows through us at all times.

In Acts 28 when Paul came to the island of Malta after a long journey resulting in a shipwreck, he was building a bonfire on the beach when a snake "fastened itself on his hand" (v. 3 NIV). Unfazed, Paul just shook it off into the fire. Instead of panicking like you or I might do when a deadly viper sinks its fangs into us, this apostle calmly shook it off. Okay, let me speak for myself: I would have been screaming and running around. But Paul knew he had the authority of the Spirit backing him up. As a result, Paul didn't break a sweat.

Seeing the snake biting Paul, the native islanders "expected him to swell up or suddenly fall dead" (v. 6 NIV). They suspected he must be a murderer or some other wicked sinner to survive a shipwreck only to have a viper bite him. Instead, they watched Paul survive and assumed he must be some kind of god. Shaking off a serious attack had its spiritual consequences, resulting in a powerful viral testimony.

SMOOTH SAILING

Paul's confidence in shaking off the snake is the same kind of powerful dependency on Jesus we can experience today. God wants us all to live within the power of His Spirit. This faith confidence reflects the reality of whom and what we are in Christ. We are called to lean forward rather than shrink back. There is an assertiveness that is expected in a follower of Jesus. The writer of Hebrews beautifully expressed this faith propulsion by referencing Habakkuk 2:4 when he said, "'Now the just shall live by faith; but if anyone draws back, my soul has no pleasure in him.' But we are not of those who draw back to perdition, but of those who believe to the saving of the soul" (Heb. 10:38–39).

Notice the contrast between people of faith and those who shrink back. The Greek word for "draw back" here is *hupostoles*, meaning literally to slack off, as in lowering a sail on a boat and therefore slowing its momentum. Leaning forward as followers of Christ, we dwell in the apostolic realm rather than what I call the "hupostolic," in which we retreat and try to play it safe and comfortable.

Because there's no middle ground, no standing still, when it comes to your spiritual journey, you're either shrinking back or advancing forward. You're hupostolic or apostolic. Your sails are up and catching the fresh breeze of the Holy Spirit, or your sails have slumped and you're drifting off course. You're engaging in faith to partner with God on an incredible spiritual adventure, or you're floating toward what you perceive as calmer, safer waters.

Those who shrink back will not access the power of God here on earth or see what is going to happen moving forward for His kingdom. If you always withdraw or hold back your heart from fully engaging with God, then you won't experience the benefits of a faith that penetrates the invisible and reveals the visible. You will not be bold or generous. You will not lead or experience miracles. You will not fulfill your divine destiny but will wander in the desert of your own desires.

If you lean into God's calling, however, then you will discover a whole new territory of uncharted spiritual adventure. If you believe in the fullness of God through Jesus Christ and expressed through the Holy Spirit, then you have a hope and a power that nothing on earth can overcome. You will naturally lead and encounter—and perform—miracles no one else could ever imagine. You will facilitate heaven on earth and witness invisible glimpses of God's heart and holiness. You will bring pleasure to your loving Father and shine with the light of His love in dark places. You will be a tour guide for heaven's glories, knowing it is your final home.

ALL NATURAL

What are the earthly, temporal actions that bring the eternal into light? They're all around us! "For since the creation of the world His invisible attributes are clearly seen, being understood by the things that are made, even His eternal power and Godhead, so that they are without excuse" (Rom. 1:20). We simply need eyes to see and ears to hear.

As followers of Jesus, we see many reflections of heavenly power and divine glory here on earth. One of the most powerful is through the practice of communion, the example Jesus asked His followers to observe at the Last Supper, on the night before His death. Partaking of the elements and blessing them as Christ instructed, we dynamically believe that the bread and wine reflect spiritual attributes when taken in faith.

The way we invest our talents and treasure can also open a doorway to heaven. We believe that our money can have kingdom power when it is given in faith. We believe that oil can bring healing when applied in faith. Many sacred rituals and spiritual practices have endured for centuries because they practice the power of God in our daily lives.

Just the power of natural beauty often broadcasts the eternal and supernatural essence of God. If you've ever breathed in the salt-scented air on the beach at sunrise, witnessed a bright green bud burst from a pale stalk, or rubbed the brindle fur of a new puppy, then you know what I'm talking about. Nature is inherently evangelistic. God's kingdom power can be witnessed in the observation of every leaf, twig, stone, wave, cloud, and canyon. God can touch people through the observance of forests, oceans, deserts, and plains. Moving in faith with natural, temporal seasons can engage heaven and open a whole new world of possibility for the rhythms of our heart. We will continue exploring the many earthly expressions of heaven's artistry throughout the chapters ahead.

DANCING LESSONS

I'm convinced that anything we do in faith moves heaven and expands God's kingdom on earth. Our spiritual power increases even more if there is a symphony of agreement with those we love. The natural world around us is waiting for our touch. When we take up the staff, the mantle, the call in faith, all of heaven moves to open the gates and send the solutions. Move! You will automatically be fulfilling your destiny and discovering your path. Your faith movements vibrate the heavens.

Perhaps instead of considering your spiritual journey with a prophetic life map, think of taking dance lessons, because discovering your prophetic life map and exploring its contours is like a dance. God gets your attention, and you either respond or discard it. He is leading the dance. As all dances go, we pick up on the nuanced signals from our partner as to direction, rhythm, tempo, and timing. Sometimes we even repeatedly dismiss impressions from heaven as coincidences. A rabbi once told me that the Hebrew language has no word for "coincidence." He spoke confidently that in God there is no such thing as coincidences. I tend to agree. It's no coincidence that you're reading this book at this time in your life.

God wants to dance with you. Will you hear the music that's playing in your life? Will you let Him lead you? Will you celebrate the marriage of Christ and the church, the union of heaven and earth? Don't settle for less than the joyful, fruitful, overflowing abundance of the Spirit-filled life. God wants to partner with you on your journey. If you open your heart, He will lead you. Let the Holy Spirit fill you with the power of knowing who you are as you draw closer to the God who made you!

YOUR VIEW FROM HERE

Disturb us, Lord, when we are too well pleased with ourselves, when our dreams have come true because we have dreamed too little, when we arrived safely because we sailed too close to the shore.
—SIR FRANCIS DRAKE, 1577

While hiking through a mountain pass or driving along a secluded coast, you can often find a place to stop and drink in the beautiful vista of your surroundings. Whether these spots offer the shade of a giant oak or the sound of a rushing waterfall nearby, they invite you to rest, gaze outward, soak inward, and savor the present moment of your journey.

At the end of each chapter, you will find a brief section intended to provide the same kind of vantage point, a place to help you make the most of your experience reading this book. This is not homework but simply an opportunity to pause, reflect, and apply the material you're engaging in these pages. These generally include a few questions for reflection, a recommended action point, and a Bible verse intended to open your conversation with God in prayer. Whether you spend a lot of time on these or a little, may you experience soul rest and a clearer perspective on where God is leading you next.

1. When have you most recently experienced a clear sense of God's presence in your life? What were the circumstances? How did He reveal Himself? How did this experience affect your relationship with Him? Why?

2. What are some of the ways you have encountered heaven on earth through the beauty of nature? What season of the year is your favorite? How does it reveal God to you and inspire you to draw closer to Him?

3. Begin planning a spiritual retreat, a time for you to be alone with God for at least one full day or longer if possible, to be taken before you complete this book. You might consider a park, café, or museum, as well as a church, retreat center, or other sacred place. For now, look at your calendar for the next month and choose a date when you will get away for this special time alone with the Lord.

The path of the just is like the shining sun,
That shines ever brighter unto the perfect day.
—PROVERBS 4:18

CHAPTER 2

YOU ARE HERE

Looking at the Pattern of Your Story

> God rewrote the text of my life when I opened
> the book of my heart to his eyes.
> —PSALM 18:24 THE MESSAGE

> Live your story or your story will live you.
> —ANONYMOUS

I'm blessed to call Cleveland, Ohio, my home.

This city has suffered greatly for the past decades and consequently has struggled to find its way forward. Once upon a time, Cleveland thrived, growing during our nation's transition from an agricultural to an industrial age, a time all about progress, steel, and production of automobiles. The city roared through the early 1900s, supported by John D. Rockefeller and other emerging millionaires bestowing wealth and prestige to this great American city. Influenced by the national "City Beautiful" movement blooming in Chicago,

Detroit, and Washington, DC, Cleveland similarly showcased stunning architecture, manicured parks, and open spaces reflecting a neoclassical aesthetic.

When the Great Depression hit following the stock market crash of 1929, Cleveland's progress slowed to a crawl. Initially, World War II delayed the decline of this beautiful gem on the shores of Lake Erie. Bolstered by the need for industrial and manufacturing operations during the war, Cleveland benefited well into the 1950s. Soon, however, it began losing out on opportunities for growth to Sunbelt cities with warmer climes and lower costs of living. Poor government leadership, unregulated standards on industrial pollution, and a host of bad breaks accelerated Cleveland's decline to the point where it became known as the "Mistake on the Lake."

WE ARE THE CHAMPIONS

Over the past thirty-plus years, I've watched this still-great city suffer from a major identity crisis. To add salt to the wound of injured pride, our professional sports teams—the Browns, the Indians, and the Cavaliers—endured a fifty-year drought without a single championship. Our teams came close to winning so many times only to collapse in a loss. Bumper stickers and T-shirts in the area even celebrated our abysmal losing streak. We just couldn't catch a break.

Until LeBron James showed up.

Rising out of nearby Akron, less than an hour south of Cleveland, this young basketball phenom immediately became a superstar, signing against all odds to play for what was virtually his hometown. LeBron soon became an ambassador of hope for Cleveland, restoring the possibility of unified joy, both on and off the court. Our wounded ego began to heal as we began shedding our old identity. New bragging rights came back to the city as we witnessed the rebirth of civic pride.

After grumbling when LeBron left us for a stint playing in Miami, most fans in Cleveland quickly forgave him when he returned because of his love for the place we all called home. Simply put, his return changed our story. In 2016, LeBron led the Cleveland Cavaliers to win the NBA Championship. At long last we finally made it to the top in sports, but what we celebrated was about much more than winning an NBA trophy. Outsiders can never understand how that win recalibrated the soul of our city.

A new tide changed the current and raised all the boats.

One person's confidence, work ethic, willpower, and goodwill began to shift the narrative for our entire city. As with all narratives, when a new story began to emerge, it rippled through the identities of every participant. Cities especially reflect the cumulative identities of its inhabitants, and ours was no different.

When a city's story begins to change, the perception of others on the outside shifts as well. And whether we like it or not, perception has power to cause change, both negative and positive. While LeBron is certainly not the singular cause of helping our city redefine itself, his passion and commitment to excellence definitely contributed. Cleveland now regularly hits top-ten lists for desirability, housing, cost of living, award-winning restaurants, and more. This great American city is on the rise again because our view of ourselves has been radically altered. Our collective narrative is changing. LeBron and the Cavs proved that we're not a mistake, not losers, not cursed. In fact, we're winners!

CHOOSE YOUR ENDING

Your story keeps unfolding until the day you die. Your narrative is made up of your choices, surprises, disappointments, innate qualities, habitual patterns, and life events both large and small. We are uniquely born into a particular family in a specific place at a definite point in temporal history, but who we are and how we live our lives are not rigidly predetermined. We are also shaped by our emerging surroundings and overall environment. Do we feel a sense of belonging? Do we feel safe? Loved? Valued? Protected? Our answers to these questions are influenced to some degree by environmental factors, both tangible and intangible.

Some of what happens is out of our control, but our responses are solely in our control. For instance, if another vehicle sideswipes us backing out of a parking space, we will probably feel an instant surge of anger, frustration, and loss. That's our immediate reaction. But how we process those emotions as we consider the situation becomes our response. In such a moment, no matter what we feel, we still choose whether we will yell and punch the other driver or act calm like a reasonable adult.

Who we become is shaped within the interiors of our heart, yet manifest in our exterior actions. We are really never without some type of choice. These choices will define what your story was, is, and will be. Our narratives are shaped by the world around us and our response to its events.

Your life is a product of your surroundings and your selections. Your narrative reflects an interaction between how you see yourself and how others in the world see you. Ultimately, your life will be navigated by the story you tell yourself. Whether you're aware of it or not, you have constructed a way of facing the world and living your life that reflects this self-narrative. But the stories we often tell ourselves are not always true.

In the Bible, the word *face* typically refers to more than just appearance. The Greek word *prosopon* appears in the Bible straight out of ancient Greek theater, where it referred to the masks actors wore to convey the emotions of the characters they portrayed. Consequently, *prosopon* includes the self-manifestation of an individual, your countenance, demeanor, attitude, and mannerisms. Simply put, your *prosopon* is usually the story others read.

Cosmetic companies, plastic surgeons, and fitness gurus would have us believe that we can control our appearance if we just spend enough, work out enough, and apply enough of the right lotions and potions to our wrinkles and scars. While there's nothing wrong with being healthy and wanting to look our best, we know that no matter how much moisturizer, concealer, or Botox we apply, the real story of our lives inevitably seeps out. One decision can affect the rest of your life.

One relationship.
One win.
One mistake.
One conversation.
One drink.
One purchase.
One glance.
One flight.
One text.

One decision can also shift you from a lifetime of doing what's right—or begin a prodigal's U-turn back toward God. Setting changes in motion, like toppling dominoes, our choices always have consequences. Poor decisions can temporarily cripple your narrative. The puzzle can become darkened, and the pieces won't fit together no matter how hard you try to force them. Godly decisions create momentum on a different trajectory, a path of contentment, purpose, fulfillment, and joy. We're all headed in one direction or the other while creating a story that's all our own.

You can choose now how your story ends later.

EPIC EXCHANGE

If you want to live out your best story, then change is essential in shaping your personal narrative. Otherwise, you will be tempted to repeat certain themes and subplots over and over again, trying to fill a void in your life that never seems full for long. Only God, our Creator, meets us in that deep place within, filling us with His love and the transformative power of His Spirit as we follow the example of His Son, Jesus. Only a life lived in Christ can change us. When you turn everything in your heart, mind, and life over to Jesus, a great exchange takes place.

You exchange your version of you for the real you, the person God created you to be. You turn in your wounds for His healing. Your distress for His peace. Your fears for His love. Your pursuits for His purposes. Your dreams for His dreams. You exchange you for Christ in you. We're told, "I have been crucified with Christ; it is no longer I who live, but Christ lives in me; and the life which I now live in the flesh I live by faith in the Son of God, who loved me and gave Himself for me" (Gal. 2:20).

Your life story becomes hidden in His. Jesus is the author and the finisher of your faith. You are now motivated to discover what is important to God and align your life with it. Your narrative is now a collaborative venture, a kind of family partnership instead of a solo. Christ's story is your story. A life that lives His testimony will bring about an epic destiny. In Revelation, John wrote about his encounter with an angel, whose beauty apparently dazzled the evangelist: "I fell at his feet to worship him. But he said to me, 'See that you do not do that! I am your fellow servant, and of your brethren who have the testimony of Jesus. Worship God! *For the testimony of Jesus is the spirit of prophecy*'" (Rev. 19:10, my emphasis).

The story and testimony of Jesus is threaded with a "spirit of prophecy," looking ahead to the future. Your future is in the story of Jesus. As you plunge your roots into Jesus and His life, you will yield uncompromised and unparalleled fruit. What you see in Jesus and His story represents and reveals the heart of God like nothing else. As you study and know Him, you understand God's ways. Your best story emerges, without a doubt, from your pursuit of Jesus. And this pursuit unfolds in your daily journey to know God and to serve Him, to explore your prophetic life map in thrilling adventures, guided and empowered by His Spirit.

God wants your story to change. He knows exactly where you are and how you got there—much better than even you know yourself. He loves and accepts you right where you are and wants more for you—more beauty, more joy, more contentment, more depth, more hope, more purpose, more substance, more peace—than you've experienced in your life so far. If you're already experiencing God's goodness, then just remember His abundance is limitless. He always has more for you.

So how can you change your story? How can you live at the heart of your real story, the only one that matters, the divine epic encompassing all of us? Become a student of Christ, a follower who grows more and more in love with the Source of all love. You dive deep into His life and God's story and embrace it as your life preserver. Once you accept the gift of His grace, once you focus only on Jesus as your life source, then life's storms no longer send you reeling. Your faith is built on bedrock, your heart is anchored by His Spirit, and you begin to walk on water!

You learn how to go with the flow.

GO WITH THE FLOW

One of the most marked-up books in my library is called *Drive*, written by Daniel Pink. Broadly speaking, it focuses on motivation.

Several of its key concepts resonated with me. One was the desire of every human being for "flow." Pink talks about how, when we are doing the ultimate of what we were carved out to do, we enter flow, a timeless sense of doing what we do best with all cylinders firing. He describes this state of clarity as satisfying and transcendent, a place where we're so deeply in the present moment that "time, place and even self melted away."[1]

I'm convinced God wants all of us to live in His flow. I suspect it's what Adam and Eve experienced in the garden. Living in God's flow means you're literally on the same page with Him. With Jesus as your Author, your story synchronizes with His supreme narrative. Flow in God brings joy and peace like nothing else. When you experience divine flow and live out of it, then you experience a deeper satisfaction, a joy that's not dependent on circumstances alone for your contentment. You're doing what you were created to do with the people you want to be with and producing fruit harvested from the trees of your dreams.

On the other hand, our sin and selfishness only hinder our flow. We start chasing our own desires instead of obeying God and doing what we know He wants us to do. We start focusing on personal pleasure and comfort instead of eternal joy and purpose. When you become entangled by your mistakes and fall into the Enemy's snares, however, you don't have to stay there. You can reclaim your flow through encounters with God and epiphanies from His Spirit.

Flow is heaven on earth. It is the thin place between the visible and invisible. It feels like nothing can go wrong and you're in the groove, hitting the spot, making the moves. It is bliss. It may not last forever, and we will still encounter difficulty on this side of heaven, but we can align ourselves to improve our consistency floating in flow.

If you're in God's flow, then even when everything around you goes south, your inward spirit holds steady to True North. This is how you can have inner peace in a raging storm. Your joy can overshadow mourning. Ashes become beautiful. Christ's flow shapes your life: "He who believes in Me, as the Scripture has said, out of his heart will flow rivers of living water" (John 7:38).

"Flow" described here springs from the confluence of a multitude of spiritual rivers. The Spirit of God carries the tide of our flow. He provides streams of strength, joy, peace, and refreshment flowing from inside of you. If you open the barriers within your heart, then the Spirit will flood your life with more streams than you can imagine. He will shape your story like waters shape the contours of a landscape.

SPY STORY

We see the power of story on full display throughout the Bible. In the Old Testament, the people of Israel endured slavery for generations until God delivered them in order to lead them home to the promised land, a lush region "flowing with milk and honey" (Ex. 3:8). Not surprisingly, their journey to the promised land can symbolize the way many of us seek God's flow for our lives. This quest represents the process of enduring depression and disappointment in the desert where we wander. It showcases the importance of obedience and trust if we're to reach the destination God has for us.

Reading in Numbers 13 we find that once the Israelites reached the promised land, their struggles didn't end. To claim and occupy their new home, they had to defeat the Canaanites, which wouldn't be easy. To assess the situation and strategize their best options, Moses sent a dozen spies into Canaan on a reconnaissance mission. When the twelve returned forty days later, two of the spies, Joshua and Caleb, reported that this place was indeed beautiful and lush, flowing with milk and honey, fertile and fruitful. As evidence, they showed some of the fruit they had brought back. They acknowledged that the inhabitants were large and strong, well armed with walled cities but had faith that God would enable them to overtake them as He had promised. Caleb concluded they should get ready to charge! The other ten saw it this way:

> But the men who had gone with him said, "We can't attack those people! They're too strong for us!" So they began to spread lies among the Israelites about the land they had explored. They said, "The land we explored is one that devours those who live there. All the people we saw there are very tall. We saw Nephilim there. (The descendants of Anak are Nephilim.) We felt as small as grasshoppers, and that's how we must have looked to them." (Num. 13:31–33 GW)

The ten negative reports shifted the perspective of a whole generation and delayed an entire nation's claim on what God had for them. Do you remember the names of Palti, Sethur, and Nahbi from the Bible? I'm guessing no one does. Why? Because they were three of the ten spies that gave the negative report. Their bodies fell in the desert, short of the promises of God. They died with the rest. They saw the same things, had the same experience, but told a very different story. They had a chance to make history but instead faded in the distance. They were offered opportunities to be champions but chose a victim mind-set and died on the wrong side of the Jordan River.

Joshua and Caleb, on the other hand, saw the possibilities and envisioned success based on God's power and faithfulness to His people. As a result, those two spies became leaders in the next phase of what God laid out. They ended up crossing over and entering the promised land. They made history and were blessed in abundance.

Their story continues to speak life into our stories today. Like them, you can live a narrative that embraces faith and hope, one that perseveres to conquer what once appeared impossible. It's a story that becomes an inspiring legacy for generations to come. You have the ability to choose the story you will tell and live out. You can give in to fear and run away from the glorious future God has for you. Or you can courageously walk by faith and allow God to revise the pages of your past into an eternal epic of redemption.

Which story will *you* tell?

BASED ON A TRUE STORY

If you want to exchange the story you've been telling yourself for God's story, then consider the various parts of your narrative. Stories typically include the following major elements: theme, plot, setting, characters, dialogue, and point of view. Let's briefly consider each of these and how they contribute to your own story. Your choices about these components ultimately calibrate the story you live out every day.

THEME

Every story has a theme, an overarching message that results from a big idea and how that big idea is conveyed. It's not enough to say a story is about love—*what* about love? If a story depicts how the love between two people allows them to endure challenging circumstances, then you're zeroing in on theme. Such a story might promote the theme that love conquers all.

How about your life story's theme? What are you all about? Where do you experience the most flow in your life? Try to sum up the theme of your life in one sentence. You might begin by considering what has consumed most of your time, attention, and energy throughout your life. Some people's lives clearly seem focused on one or two big areas, such as education, career, work, marriage, friends, family, sports, finance, travel, or community service. Other people's lives seem to weave several big priorities into their thematic fabric.

After you identify one or two key areas at the center of your life, describe your relationship to them. Are you sacrificing marriage and a family to focus on a successful career? Do your kids come first above everything else no matter what? Is your commitment to serving in your local church driving your schedule each week? As you consider the likely theme of your life right now, ask yourself an even more important question: Is this what you want your life to be known for? Greater still, is this what God wants your life to be known for?

PLOT

Next, consider your life story's plot. Fiction writers usually consider plot to include the major events in a story as well as their relationship to each other and other parts of the story. In a mystery novel, it's not just that someone killed someone else. It's also about why they killed someone else, which means that the detective must investigate not only the forensic clues and factual details but also the motives of all the characters involved to identify what really happened.

If you think of your life as a kind of mystery, what are the main events that have had the greatest impact, both good and bad, on your life? Consider looking at your life based on ages and stages to give you a handle on these events, such as childhood, adolescence, early adulthood, full-blown adulthood, middle age, and so on. Take time to write down your main events and see if there are patterns or relationships among them. Did one event contribute to another happening? Have you made certain choices in life in response to painful losses or personal traumas? When did your life seem to take a new or unexpected direction? When have you seen God intervene or reveal Himself in your life? What moments tilted you in dangerous directions? Where are you now in relation to these key events?

SETTING

The setting of a story reflects both time and place, when and where it occurs. You can see the important role setting plays in a story by comparing historical fiction to a contemporary novel to a sci-fi futuristic epic. Simply put, our relationship to time and place matter! Physical settings affect the geography of our souls.

What is the setting for your story? Where did your life begin, and where have you traveled to get to where you live now? When people ask, "Where are you from?" what do you say? Are you more at home in a small town or an inner city? In the US Midwest or the global Far East? Do you prefer mountains or beaches? Sidewalks or trails? Where do you feel most alive? Where do you get the sense you belong? What time periods fascinate you most? How do you view the current time in which you live?

CHARACTERS

Every play has characters at the center of its story. Who are your main characters? Who are the people who have shaped your life with the greatest impact? Who influenced you growing up? And who influences you the most now? In addition to family and close friends, who are the people you love being around who stir your soul? The fifth-century Celtic Christians called these *anam cara,* or "soul friends." You know, the kind of friends who leave you a better person than when you arrived. They pour into your life and nourish your spirit. They never drain you or steer you in a negative direction. They are lifters.

You can't always choose your family members nor your work associates, but you can select the people with whom you're willing to engage your heart. I've heard people say, "Show me your five closest friends and I can predict your future." There is some truth to that statement. The main characters in your life will shape your thinking whether you like it or not. Because our relationships influence so much of our lives, we'll explore more about them in chapters to come. For now, simply consider how you would describe each of the main people in your life.

DIALOGUE

Characters in our stories influence us by what they do as well as by what they say. Dialogue includes the important conversations, lingering words, and repeated phrases that become the vocabulary of our souls. What do you spend most of your time talking about? What words from a parent, teacher, or coach haunt you from childhood? Who speaks words of encouragement and support to you on a regular basis? What words do you most regret saying to others? The Bible tells us that the tongue has incredible power as the source of the words we speak. Words can cut and kill, or they can soothe and heal. They can express love and acceptance or scorch and scar your soul.

POINT OF VIEW

Next, your point of view will be first person. We are each the hero or heroine of our stories. We see everything and everyone else around us in relation to who we are and how we see ourselves. That means you are the author of the story, telling this epic tale of your existence in your daily thoughts as well as your milestone memories. You have the right to share your story if you own it.

Teaching a business course for many years, my colleagues and I have helped improve people's public speaking by a simple method: only share stories you have earned the right to talk about. When you share your story as honestly and authentically as possible, it will be yours and yours alone, no matter how similar it might be to someone else's. If you don't contrive the way you tell it or try to imitate someone else's story, then you will always have a story worth telling.

NOT THE END

Identifying the story you've been telling yourself is the first step toward changing it. And if you're already allowing God to author your narrative, then reviewing it allows you to experience more and more flow from His Spirit. It's important to remember where you've come from in order to know how to move forward to where you're going.

God will continue to show you the way, if you let Him. If you open the book of your heart, then He will revise your story into one of miraculous redemption with the ultimate happy ending: being in heaven with Him forever. The Holy Spirit can help you author the most amazing life possible. He is flow. When you walk in the Spirit by faith, you begin to live out the best story possible.

No matter where you are in your life, no matter how old or young, how rich or poor, how lonely or overwhelmed, your story is not over. It's never too late to start a new chapter or experience the most wonderful, unexpected plot twist. If you're willing to see your story through God's eyes, then the best is yet to come!

YOUR VIEW FROM HERE

There is no greater agony than bearing an untold story inside you.

—MAYA ANGELOU

1. Based on where you are at this point in your life, which genre best reflects your story? Action-adventure? Romantic comedy? Documentary? Western? Superhero

saga? Thriller? Something else? Why would you classify your story this way?

2. Of the six story elements mentioned—theme, plot, setting, characters, dialogue, and point of view—which element in your own story resonates the most with you right now? Why? How would you want to change this particular story element?

3. After spending some time in prayer reflecting on how God may want to speak to you through the ideas in this chapter, schedule time in the next week to meet with an *anam cara*—a soul friend, family member, or trusted believer, preferably someone who knows you well—for a meal or coffee. Ask this person to help you look at your story, both the one you've been telling yourself most of your life as well as the one you know God is calling you to live. Conclude your time by praying together as God's Spirit leads you.

"For I know the plans I have for you," declares the LORD, "plans to prosper you and not to harm you, plans to give you hope and a future."

—JEREMIAH 29:11 NIV

CHAPTER 3

MAP READING

Planning Your Future

A man's heart plans his way,
But the LORD directs his steps.
—PROVERBS 16:9

Don't wait for your ship to come in—swim out
to it!
—ANONYMOUS

When I was twenty-three, my mentor challenged me to write out a life plan. I took his assignment seriously and planned out my life up until age eighty-five. When I shared my life plan the next time we met, he seemed amused by my level of detail. Apparently, he expected only broad strokes of the life I imagined, while I produced something quite specific. Embarrassed then, over time I've been amazed at how closely my life has followed this plan.

For example, in my imagined trajectory, I included a trip to Australia at age thirty-eight, which seemed rather random at the time. Sure enough, though, when I was thirty-eight, I unexpectedly began to receive invitations to speak in Australia, resulting in eight trips there within five years!

I have often pondered that exercise completed when I was a young man. Did God put it in my heart regarding my future, or did He look at my plan and say, "Let's do it"? Either way, planning and casting a vision for my life has shaped the direction it has taken.

TAKE AIM

Few of us would haphazardly venture on a trip or vacation without a map or plan. Similarly, as you discover and utilize your prophetic life map, you need to know where you are going in order to set your course for that destination. Someone once said, "Aim at nothing and you're sure to hit it." If we don't think about where and how we want to finish, then it's much more likely to drift on the current of circumstances or default to the decisions of others.

As followers of Jesus, the target for our faith is to finish well. We all want to stand before God and hear, "Well done, good and faithful servant!" (Matt. 25:21 NIV). Toward the end of his life, the apostle Paul declared, "I have fought the good fight, I have finished the race, and I have kept the faith" (2 Tim. 4:7).

Our temporal and eternal lives are summed up in this verse. We are in a fight to the end, a race to the finish, and we want to finish strong. A heavenly reward awaits us for our labors. Our desire to please the Lord gives us a second wind. We do all we do in order to experience the eternal fulfillment of our divine legacy.

Jesus said, "Which of you, intending to build a tower, does not sit down first and count the cost, whether he has enough to finish it" (Luke 14:28). We are called to assess and count the cost. I believe in constant assessment in this life to create course corrections when necessary. I don't want my life ending up somewhere I didn't intend or that's out of line with where God wants to take me. We want to cooperate with God for the best outcome. That's why we must speak with Him constantly and pay attention to the many ways He communicates with us.

As we consider how to find direction for our lives, it's important to consider how we want to finish our journey on this earth. We explore our dreams in order to construct our future. Your dreams provide the key to knowing where you're going, and your plans provide the map for how you're going to get there.

PLANS REQUIRE FAITH

There's something powerful about imagining your future.

Such an exercise can be taken to extremes, though. Planning your future is scorned in certain parts of the church because we're told to focus only on today, while in the world at large, vision casting is often idolized. In between such extremes, however, a plan is simply a dream with a deadline. Planning is meant to be the servant of the vision, not vice versa.

Sometimes the process of moving toward a dream is dynamically initiated by God, and at other times it begins as a burden of the heart, a compelling urgency from within. Undoubtedly, we can say the burden was placed in our heart by God, and therefore nothing of the kingdom doesn't begin outside of heaven. In other words, what appears to be our idea is only the latent discovery of God's true intention for our moving forward. Nevertheless, planning your life's path, while knowing your route will be diverted, allows you to set goals and work hard, while also relying on God's ongoing guidance and direction.

The way I see it, planning is an act of faith. When you plan, you're saying that you believe in this dream enough to give time, energy, and money to make it happen. The combination of thinking, planning, and acting demonstrates to heaven that you're serious in your intention. You're taking steps as if your vision is really going to come to life.

God's Word explains, "Faith is the substance of things hoped for, the evidence of things not seen" (Heb. 11:1). Shifting your life to move toward something hoped for but not presently seen definitely requires faith. Enrolling in school to complete your education is an act of faith as you imagine holding your diploma someday. Going on a date is an act of faith as you keep the hope in your heart alive with the dream of a loving spouse. Cleaning out your garage in order to put your home up for sale requires faith that someday soon there will be a Sold sign in your yard.

Who you are and how you live is a tangible expression of what you really believe. Guarding your dream by not selling it short or taking a quick but questionable route is an act of faith. Monitoring your friends and involvements so as to protect your dream exercises faith. Are you on the path to your God-given dreams? Do you have a plan for how to get there? Is it measurable? Do your daily actions move you closer to this heavenly vision of your future?

SEE YOUR SEASONS

An easy way to begin thinking about how to make a map for the rest of your life is to "begin with the end in mind," as Stephen Covey urges in *The 7 Habits of Highly Effective People*.[1] Imagine your life as you reach your ninetieth birthday and look back. What would you see? Or think about how your eulogy would read after finishing a long, productive life. When I teach leadership training, I often have students imagine the rest of their lives and then write their own eulogies to summarize their vision. Often one of the most powerful exercises you can complete, writing your own eulogy forces you to look long and hard at where you are right now and where you want to be—and, therefore, how you're going to get there.

For the sake of convenience, I encourage you to consider your life in three segments of thirty years each: from birth to thirty, from thirty to age sixty, and from age sixty to ninety. In the first third of your life, there's a sense of growing, learning, and beginning. It's no accident that Joseph, David, and Jesus entered into public service at age thirty after having been prepared by experiences in their first three decades. Similarly, you may have learned much from your training and formal education but lack the experience that comes from actually doing what God has equipped you to do.

The second span of thirty years is often focused on doing, trying, working, running, and persevering. This is when you take what you know and gain experience. Experience can be equal to or greater than book knowledge in some fields. Your financial engine tends to increase during this second section of life, your key earning years. For many people, this span is also the season for marriage and family building. Many life lessons are learned as your soul gets shaped and crafted by the Master Potter.

Finally, your third season focuses on your legacy. This is the time that you are hopefully enjoying the fruits of your labor and transitioning your legacy of wisdom, wealth, and wonder to another generation. These truly can be the golden years, the pinnacle of your life's pursuit of your divine path. Perhaps no other season, however, relies on planning as much as this final third of your life.

FACE YOUR FUTURE

Whether you use these three categories or your own, I urge you to map out your life on paper. Perhaps you've done it before, but it never hurts to update your previous plans. Feel free to write, draw, doodle, sketch—whatever feels helpful as you attempt to cast a vision for where you're going. Writing your own eulogy, perhaps start with writing a paragraph that summarizes your response to each of the following questions:

Who was I?
What did I do?
What did I leave?

If this exercise feels overwhelming or depressing, then keep it simple. As you try to describe who you are and who you want to be, start by listing words that describe you or that are meaningful to you. For example, mine include: lover of God, wife, family, motorcycles, coffee, travel, Italy, books, writing, beach, mountains, and water, just to name a few. What would other people say about you that would be unique or descriptive of you? Write those down too. This paragraph sets a preferred future for who you're becoming. It describes how you want others to remember you, the kind of person you are, and the role you played in their lives.

Next, think about what you want to be known for doing. This involves your day-to-day actions, accomplishments, and activities, as well as any major achievements, recognitions, or honors bestowed during your life. Allow your mind to dream about the totality of all your endeavors. How do you want to be remembered? What are the temporal and eternal goals you want to accomplish in your lifetime? What does it look like for you to finish well? Again, just to give you an example, mine would include planting and building up churches, coaching and mentoring others, and writing books to share the wisdom God has revealed to me.

Your third and final paragraph describes the eternal impact you will leave on this earth. It speaks to the people, accomplishments, and endeavors you invested in most. What will last and transcend your time here? For my life, I want to be known as someone who invested in the lives of others and helped them experience more of the grace, love, and power of God. I want to be remembered as a risk taker, an adventurer, someone who kept his feet on the ground and his eyes on heaven.

After you've come up with a response to all three main questions, put them together to form your eulogy. Here's what mine looks like:

Steve was a thoughtful, engaging, enthusiastic person who loved to drink coffees and travel to new places and passionately know Jesus. He enjoyed a life of adventure with his wife, Cindy, four children, and many grandchildren. He was a risk taker, motivator, and cultivator of people around the world. He was a creative dreamer and finished what he began.

Living well into his nineties, Steve is survived by three daughters and a son, numerous grandchildren, and a wife of seventy years. Churches were built and established in several countries. He was responsible for the digging of hundreds of water wells in Africa. The winning of souls became his passion in later life and countless conversions were recorded worldwide.

Steve reached his goal of writing ten books, including a bestselling novel, which continues to inspire and delight readers. Friends were made around the world, with special ones in Canada and England. He leaves a legacy of a storyteller, pastor, and friend.

Yours will naturally be unique to your experiences so far, but don't limit yourself based on what seems logical or probable. Dream big! Focus on the broad strokes, but feel free, just like I did at age twenty-three, to make it as detailed as you wish. Hold on to this plan and then revisit it at regular intervals. Revise it and add to it. Let it be shaped by new relationships, new adventures, and new goals. Ask God to move in you and through you as you pursue actualizing this vision of your life.

Will your life follow this plan? Not necessarily—or maybe not at all. But thinking, reflecting, imagining, and committing it to paper will begin to reveal where God might be leading you next. Creating a written plan of what you hope your life will look like allows you to move in directions that will realize your dreams.

PLAN THE WORK, WORK THE PLAN

Once you have a plan, then it becomes a matter of how to actualize it. Just as measuring miles allows you to reach your destination, setting attainable goals provides similar milestones for measuring your progress. They are demarcation points that allow you to look ahead and yet glance back to assure yourself of continued progress. Without breaking your dreams into smaller steps, you may become tempted to focus on what appears to be impossible, unlikely, or improbable instead of relying on God.

In the Bible, Nehemiah faced such a dilemma. Burdened to rebuild the ruined walls of Jerusalem, Nehemiah, however, was in a society that limited his movement. Functioning basically as a slave, he was severely restricted in his ability to fulfill the vision he had for restoration. Nonetheless, he apparently thought and planned based on "what if?" As a result, he was prepared when the king said, "What is it you want?" (Neh. 2:4 NIV). Nehemiah's response demonstrated deep thought and precise planning. His method could be a lesson for any planner today. Here is a breakdown of Nehemiah's method based on his requests and subsequent actions:

CAST A CLEAR AND PRECISE VISION

Nehemiah was direct. He told the king, "Send me to Judah to rebuild the city" (Neh. 2:5 NLT). People tend to ramble when asked about their dreams. Key authorities that have the power to fulfill your plans need quick and clear understanding. Some people call this the elevator speech. It's a clear summation of a dream. Give prayerful thought to your destiny statement.

ANTICIPATE QUESTIONS

How long? When will you return? These are good basic questions that many are not prepared to answer. Nehemiah was. He had thought through the process and had answers ready for the proper moment. A well-thought-out dream gives you ammunition for an expanded conversation. Have you traveled down the corridors of your dream to explore potential challenges and how to solve them? Start thinking through the who, what, when, where, how, and why of your dream. Nehemiah did!

SET A TIMELINE

Nehemiah set a timeline for the king (v. 6). The ability to put time values on a project is essential. Setting deadlines creates expectations and makes planning possible with other moving pieces. With any quote I get from a contractor, I also want a timeline. How long will it take you to complete this project, and what is your deadline? Think through your life. What will be needed to accomplish the dream on your heart, and how long will it take? What type of education will you need, and who are the people you need to put in your path to assist you in realizing your goals?

Pray. Think. Plan. Remember, when I was twenty-three years old, I set a timeline for my life that continued until age eighty-five!

GET ACCESS

Nehemiah knew the king's authority and influence and quickly requested the proper documentation for his journey (vv. 7–8). Being a cupbearer to the king, Nehemiah observed how the king's business worked on a day-to-day basis. He asked for materials to make the project work (v. 8). The king also provided letters that gave Nehemiah protection and authority (vv. 7–8). While it's great to want to do things all by yourself, nobody is truly "self-made." God will use many people to assist you on your journey. Don't be afraid to ask for assistance along the way, especially from mentors, friends, family, and authorities. You must be ready to move in boldness and declare what you need to fulfill your vision.

LIMIT SHARING THE VISION

In Jerusalem, Nehemiah rose in the night to scope out the project, and was careful to tell only appropriate people of his intentions (v. 16). Little did he know that the seeds of obstruction were already being sown in the hearts of two men. They would become his harassers but also would be used to continue to mature Nehemiah into a true leader. If you recall, when Joseph shared his dreams to his brothers, he ended up misunderstood, despised, and living in a pit. Internet social sites have emerged as quick killers to dreams and visions. Learn to limit your communications, and keep a small group of confidants. Nehemiah traveled and planned by night in order to not arouse enemies (v. 13). Select carefully what you post on the internet. You may be slowly recruiting your enemies.

KNOW THE RIGHT TIME TO SPEAK UP

Nehemiah was bold to speak when it came time. His prophetic words of encouragement aroused a weary people, and they repeated back exactly what he had said. He was now committed. There is no turning back. You can't confess a dream and raise the hopes of people if you continue to abort your vision. Hold your moment until the right time, but when it comes, speak with confidence. Consider how Peter, after denying his connection with Jesus just weeks prior, on the day of Pentecost took his stand and raised his voice. Practice your speech and envision your comrades.

NEVER GIVE UP

When you finally find the groove of fulfillment, don't hand it off, compromise it, or get talked out of it. Nehemiah had great opposition from those who first tried with words to discourage him and later tried with life threats. He ended up working with a tool in one hand and a weapon in the other. When his detractors tried to get him off task he said: "I am doing a great work, so that I cannot come down. Why should the work cease while I leave it and go down to you?" (Neh. 6:3).

SET SMART GOALS

As we see with Nehemiah, working a plan requires setting goals. While it's often easier to set goals rather than reach them, most plans won't get off the ground without setting smaller goals. In the business world, I used to teach about how to set SMART goals. Created by George T. Doran, SMART is the acronym for Specific, Measurable, Attainable, Relevant, and Time-phased. Goals give you direction. Goals keep you focused, and goals help you chart your progress. A SMART goal gives you clarity by defining your objective and plotting the shortest and most efficient path to it.

For example, if I have a goal of becoming a doctor, I will have to activate shorter incremental goals of schooling, residency, and so forth. I create bite-size chunks that work me toward the destination. I call these goals that benefit you in this life "role goals." They reflect your emerging role as a husband, wife, business owner, parent, teacher, mentor, and so on. They help you achieve what is expected from others based on your response to your life's purpose and God's calling.

Role goals enhance us horizontally. They improve our horizons. They are deployed in order to increase our external realm. They are action and movement oriented and reveal what steps need to be taken in order to fulfill the responsibilities of the role. They assess how we can best serve and measure success in terms we can typically see and measure. The Bible says, "The plans of the diligent lead surely to plenty, but those of everyone who is hasty, surely to poverty" (Prov. 21:5).

The other kind of goals, which I call "soul goals," focus more on eternal investments, although they may include benefits here on earth as well. Soul goals can be a place of development and maturity versus a place of measured accomplishment. These are the goals that enhance your vertical and internal quality of life, such as practicing ways to experience more joy, peace, and security. While these tend to be more abstract and intangible, they can still fulfill the SMART qualities.

This is not intended to be a legalistic journey. It's about aligning yourself with Jesus through inner focus on the development of your soul. It's a journey of desire for more of God. It has an intrinsic understanding of our need of the grace of God; otherwise, it's just a self-help mission. Soul goals are the observed intangibles. They create habits that are more Christlike. They look to the future and ask, "Am I being conformed into the image of Jesus?" Soul goals are prophetic benchmarks as opposed to natural destinations. How am I aligning myself with what God has spoken over me? They are places where you want to be in Christ.

Soul goals also address "What will the condition of my soul be in one year?" Other possible goals could be, "What fruit of the Spirit do I want shaped in me over the next year?" I use *year* in these examples because they offer a cultural measuring rod. At the beginning of a new year or on a birthday would be optimal times to create a soul goal. What would it be like to write these down and then craft a plan to create an environment of soul change? It is a plan to move in cooperation with the Holy Spirit to improve the temple of living stones that we are being built into. It is prophetic in nature. Be careful how you build. We need to seek gold, silver, and precious stones in anything we pursue. Wood, hay, and stubble are too vulnerable to fire.

MASTERY AND MYSTERY

The plans of Christians, while just as smart as anyone else's, must remain more fluid. No matter how carefully or thoughtfully we plan, we must continually rely on God and His Spirit for our direction each day. Only God is all knowing and all powerful. Even when we prophesy, we do so only in part while He sees the biggest picture of all. Therefore, we plan knowing He may cause our route to change.

While this process is inherently supernatural, the following diagram illustrates how we plan and how God interprets those plans. In other words, He doesn't always take the same route we do! See the arrow to the left.

This is where you have your aha moment. This is where your dream is downloaded or initiated. Too often, we're trained to seek the fastest and easiest way to the concluding point at the left.

The path of the Holy Spirit is more fluid. He will take you on the ride of your life. It always reminds me of the rhythm of a washing machine: the ups and downs, backward and forward of motion are meant to bring cleansing. Sounds about right! Everything above the horizontal line in the chart speaks of the manifestation of fruitfulness. In that section, God speaks *through* you. It tends to be more visible and public. The curving line of the Holy Spirit has scattered prophecies that come up in your spiritual life. They give you the line of sight to your destiny. It is a faith- and confidence-building time. You have soaring vision, understand your call, and feel that finally progress is being made. Then the roller coaster speeds downward.

SPIRIT PATH CHART

MANIFEST OUT FLOW DO FRUIT

GOD SPEAKS THROUGH ME!

VISION DESTINY IDENTITY CALLING

MASTERY

MORE LORD!

HIDDEN IN EBB BE PRUNE

GOD SPEAKS IN ME!

MYSTERY

CONSOLIDATE ENCOURAGE RECALIBRATE BUILD

LEGEND

— Preferred Path

Holy Spirit Path

Spirit-Led Goals [Soul Goals]

Holy Spirit opens new path

Prophetic Words

Prophetic Line of Sight

Goals intersect with the Spirit Path

Below the line is more of a hidden place. God starts to speak strongly *in* you. In times like this, you consolidate, recalibrate, and take inventory on who you are and your relationship to God. It can be triggered by difficulty, crisis, or just a change in your personal or surrounding climate. Nonetheless, it's an important time. Your future depends on your response versus your reaction. Learn, be pruned, and bear greater fruit.

The bold vertical lines are goals that you set. These goals are possibly role goals and soul goals. As you see from the chart, goals may be reached at different times and places, but I still believe they are important. Goals keep you focused and continue to energize you toward the fulfillment of the dream.

Above the line, you *acquire mastery*. Below the line, you *understand mystery*. The Holy Spirit will shape you and mold you. When you arrive at your destination, you are changed. You will not feel the same. You are fuller, stronger, and more dependent on God.

We see this process illustrated in the way David pursued the plans of the temple with an understanding of cooperation between heaven and earth: "Then David gave his son Solomon the plans for the vestibule, its houses, its treasuries, its upper chambers, its inner chambers, and the place of the mercy seat; and the plans for all that he had by the Spirit, of the courts of the house of the LORD" (1 Chron. 28:11–12). Note the "plans by the Spirit"!

You, too, are the temple of the Lord, the precious dwelling place for His Spirit. He has a plan for your life that is being created right now as you read the words on this page. So plan as if you are a partner with the Holy Spirit—because you are!

YOUR VIEW FROM HERE

Organizing is what you do before you do something,
so that when you do it, it is not all mixed up.
—A. A. MILNE

1. When you consider planning your life, how do you feel? Excited? Overwhelmed? Afraid? Unsettled? Worried? Eager? Something else? Why do you think you feel this way? How would you like to feel as you look ahead and plan your life?

2. What plan are you currently following in your life? What goals have you set for this year? Just as we're likely to spend more money than we earn without a budget, we're just as likely to lose focus on where God wants to lead us without a plan. What's one goal you can set for this week to help you move forward with crafting or updating your life plan?

3. If you haven't written your eulogy yet, spend a few minutes drafting three short paragraphs that identify who you were, what you did, and what will last from the life you lived. What's the single biggest change you need to make in order to move in a direction that aligns with the eulogy you hope to have at the end of your life?

Now listen, you who say, "Today or tomorrow we will go to this or that city, spend a year there, carry on business and make money." Why, you do not even know what will happen tomorrow. What is your life? You are a mist that appears for a little while and then vanishes. Instead, you ought to say, "If it is the Lord's will, we will live and do this or that."
—JAMES 4:13–15 NIV

CHAPTER 4

TRAILBLAZING

Glimpsing God on Your Journey

For now we see in a mirror, dimly, but then face
to face. Now I know in part, but then I shall
know just as I also am known.
—I CORINTHIANS 13:12

Nature is the art of God.
—DANTE

A few years ago, I was having doubts about the direction my life was taking. While I was following the God-plan for my life, my efforts didn't appear to be producing the fruit I expected. Then I had a dream that seemed to speak into my frustration.

In my dream, I was talking to a well-known, successful pastor, someone I had never actually met in the waking world. While this dream had many parts, the most significant occurred when this pastor told me, "Read Hadid." I had no idea what he meant in my dream or when I woke up the next morning. Who or what was *Hadid*? To the best I could recall, I had never heard of it before.

So I went online and Googled *Hadid* only to discover the name of a world-renowned British architect. Famous for her deconstructionist designs that seem to liberate geometry, Zaha Hadid was considered one of the best architects in the world, the "queen of curve." Prior to her death in 2016, she had designed numerous iconic buildings, museums, and special-event venues, including the aquatic center in London for the 2012 Olympics and a World Cup soccer stadium still under construction in Qatar.[1] In article after article I read about her, one detail stood out: Hadid's work always focused on futuristic bold curves.

Then I understood.

My dream was not specifically about this woman's life or spiritual beliefs—the message emerged in her style of work, her aesthetic. Symbolically, God was telling me to move ahead in "futuristic bold curves." And it wasn't as crazy as it might sound, because such an idea had already been planted in my mind. Visiting a church in California a few weeks before, I received a prophetic word from a complete stranger during one of the services. That woman knew nothing about me but came right over and described a vision from God. She said I was a train being transformed from a steam engine to a bullet train. She saw me speeding toward a long, lush curve into my destiny in God!

Without a doubt, I know this word and my dream were from God. As He continues to guide me, He orders up multiple revelations to direct me. Knowing I was to continue in the same direction and that my life's momentum was picking up speed, I felt a renewed confidence and power to move forward. Thanks to God's use of a British architect's style and the faithful word delivered by a messenger in California, I knew. Now I had hope, direction, and a clearer picture of the spiritual destiny God was creating in me!

DREAM CATCHER

My experience, while unique to my life, is not unusual. God speaks to all of us throughout our lives in various ways—including our dreams. Dreams are a popular vehicle in the Bible, yet they have been minimized by modern thinking. If we're paying attention and allowing God to speak through them, dreams can reveal a key message or next direction. Our dreams often reinforce and echo important themes or reveal instructions for how God wants us to proceed.

We see this pattern throughout the Bible. In the Old Testament book of Genesis, after Joseph was falsely imprisoned, his ability to interpret dreams became the ticket to his destiny (chap. 41). Curiously enough, it was the dream he had as a young man—and the blunt interpretation he shared with his jealous brothers—that landed him in Egypt in the first place. Perhaps over the years, Joseph learned to deliver his interpretation with more tact and diplomacy; he impressed Pharaoh enough to become his second-in-command.

In the New Testament, another Joseph, Mary's fiancé, was told in a dream not to fear marrying the young virgin who was carrying a child that he knew was not his own (Matt. 1:20). This divine assurance eliminated any doubts that he might have had regarding the direction of his future. An honorable man, Joseph was willing to break the engagement quietly until this message compelled him to move forward and take Mary as his wife. This is a destiny dream.

Joseph also received another vital message through a dream, this time to take Mary and baby Jesus to Egypt in order to escape King Herod's murderous decree (Matt. 2:13). They fled south and remained there until Joseph was told in yet another dream that Herod had died, so it was safe to return to Israel (v. 19). Three major decisions in Joseph's life were all directed by dreams. This carpenter from Nazareth became a loving husband and devoted father to the Son of God because he listened to God's voice echoing in his dreams. God led him by using one of the most powerful, grace-filled means of revelation—one He still uses in our lives today.

God is interested in your destiny. He desires to direct you along the way. He will choose a number of means to inspire, convince, and/or direct you to that end. Dreams are one of the ways He gets our attention, but if we're paying attention, we will discover other "spiritual bread crumbs" on the path leading us home.

LEAD THE WAY

Even as we follow our plans and pursue our divine destination, we must be willing to trail blaze into new territory as His Spirit leads us. These detours are usually unexpected and may catch us unprepared, especially if life had been going according to plan. But we must not fear such times when God suddenly reveals Himself or shows us a new direction.

In addition to our collaborative life plan, clues about how we should proceed often abound if we keep our eyes open and our ears attuned to God's voice. Never underestimate the importance of being aware and valuing all revelation based in Jesus. Eight times in the book of Revelation we read, "Whoever has ears, let them hear" (NIV). Clearly, God will speak to us if we're willing to listen. If we have committed our whole lives to God, then we must be willing to listen as we seek Him along the way.

Sometimes, we follow and obey His voice before we realize what He's up to—especially if He seems to be leading us off-road. For example, years ago I was asked to speak at a large evangelical church. I was surprised because I had no relational or denominational connection and couldn't see why they would invite me. I wasn't even sure they would agree with much of what I believe about the Spirit of God. Nevertheless, I went.

While I think my message was well received, it was right after the service that I discovered the real reason I was there. A lovely older lady approached me in the crowded lobby and abruptly asked me if I was the speaker that day. When I confirmed that I was, she immediately asked, "Would you ever want to come to the Bahamas and speak?" Indicating my willingness (I remember thinking, *Who wouldn't!*), I asked her to give me the info, promising to check it out and get back to her. "I've gotta tell you," she smiled and said, "if you're not any good, we won't have you back!"

"I'll do my best," I told her, confident that she was not kidding.

A few months later, I ended up in the Bahamas. After speaking the first Sunday, however, I discovered the real reason this woman had invited me down. Outside of the gated resort where I was staying, a group of Haitian refugees lived in poverty. Many didn't have homes, but together they had built a little church—one with walls but no roof. My hostess had hoped I would catch her vision to help them, both through my preaching but also by providing assistance with physical needs, like the roof. After my first visit to their church, I was fully on board.

With the help of my good friend and business mentor, Bob Knight, along with a great local team, the roof was installed within six months—just before they braced for a hurricane. That church building has served as a spiritual center as well as a community gathering place ever since.

I have now been going to that same area for more than ten years, and it serves as a place of great refreshment and many friendships. The Lord used a meandering path of connection and divine happenstance to fulfill the needs of many people whose paths might not have intersected otherwise. He does the same for you.

God has a plan for you. Some of it will be clear and logical. Much of it will surprise you along the way.

DELIGHT AND DESIRE

Once we're committed to knowing God and following Him as the Spirit leads, then how do we know the direction of our lives if everything's not going according to plan? How do we dream into a future that has so many unknowns and seems to change continually? How can we follow the twists and turns of life and still bring our God-given dreams to life?

There's no easy answer or simple set of one-size-fits-all directions. Discovering and following your prophetic life map is not a science as much as it is an art. As we collaborate with God to fulfill the potential of the beautiful life He has given us, we experience the abundance Jesus told us He came to bring. Simply put, the process of our journey matters as much as the destination.

Your destiny is designed by God and built by you. It will have an aesthetic, a shape, a pattern with details uniquely your own. Like the sweeping curves of a building designed by Zaha Hadid, your prophetic life map reveals something fluid, intricate, and entirely your own. It will have color, texture, taste, feel, shape, and size. While we have a say in how it's constructed as we move forward, we also have a loving Father willing to guide us. We have nothing to fear as we step out in faith and follow Him, discovering the surprise He has for us around the next corner while pursuing the dreams He has placed in our hearts.

Our life in the Spirit is directed by God in us, but we're not robots. Our Creator gives us free will to choose how we will respond to His love and His call on our lives. Based on our response, we grow closer and closer to Him as we become more authentically who He made us to be even as we become more like His Son, Jesus. Or, we choose not to listen to His voice as we pursue distractions and detours that result in dead ends. Every choice we make each day moves us in a certain direction—one that we hope brings us closer to God and all that He has for us.

Praying and reading God's Word are the primary ways we converse with Him and learn to recognize His voice. We're told, "My sheep hear My voice, and I know them, and they follow Me. And I give them eternal life, and they shall never perish; neither shall anyone snatch them out of My hand" (John 10:27–28). In addition to speaking to our hearts as we pray and listen, the Lord continually communicates to us through the Bible, revealing His righteous paths and ways to live that honor Him. If we follow His wisdom and obey His commands, then preferable outcomes arise as a result of our partnership. We're told, "Delight yourself also in the LORD, and He shall give you the *desires of your heart* (Ps. 37:4, my emphasis). If we delight in knowing and following God, then our hearts' desires are aligned with His plan for our lives.

Any message we receive or think we receive will never violate the truth of God's Word. If we receive or interpret such a message in a way that seems to contradict His character, then it is most likely not from Him. God speaks into our lives to give us good gifts that enhance our ability to serve Him and fulfill the purpose for which He created us. His Spirit is never going to guide us to sin or intentionally harm others. While our lives may not be easy or even comfortable in the ways we might prefer, we can trust that God is for us. He wants our ultimate best, and His plans for us are filled with joy, peace, and purpose.

GOD'S GUIDEPOSTS

As I consider the many other ways in addition to prayer and God's Word that He guides us, I come back to the Celtic traditions and their emphasis on what I interpret as "soul nouns"—the people, places, and things that enrich our spiritual lives and provide direction from God. Through them, the Lord often reveals Himself and His direction for our lives, perhaps through a surprising conversation, a sunrise on the beach, or a book that seems to speak right to our present need.

Just think about the people in your life who have had the greatest spiritual impact. As we discussed in the previous chapter, these individuals, whom the Celts called *anam cara*, or "soul friends," enhance, enliven, and enrich your life in countless ways. They get you. They accept you and they like you. Best of all, they love you unconditionally and reflect God's love to you. They may live next door or in another country, but when you get with them, your connection instantly closes the gaps of geography or the time that passed since your last visit. You pick right up where you left off, eager to share, and to know and be known. These people are some of God's most precious gifts in your life.

Obviously, one of these persons can and should be your spouse. But your soul tribe goes beyond any one person. They're people with whom you quickly bond and experience a natural, unforced rhythm in relationship. Mutual growth occurs when you get together. You feel that heaven is near when they are present. Soul friends help you shape your destiny and reveal opportunities.

I'm blessed by some amazing friends I've known for almost three decades. They love me for who I am, and when we get together, we're free to be ourselves. We share a sense of humor at life's absurdities as well as a sense of wonder at its beauty and mystery. We often laugh at strange things at strange hours. We share life experiences together and grow deeper in our commitment to one another. We share life, the ups and downs and in-betweens, even if only in short increments.

Who are the soul friends in your life right now? Invest in these relationships and listen to the wisdom God imparts through them. They're often part of your journey for many years, if not your entire lifetime. If nothing else, a sense of belonging and protection results from these friends. Author and Celtic scholar John O'Donohue wrote in his book *Eternal Echoes*, "Nowhere do we feel so deeply encountered as we do in the presence of another human being."[2] After all, God said that it was not good to be alone.

THIN PLACES

We also find direction for our life through sacred places, what the Celts often called "thin places" because they seem closer to heaven than others. In fact, these thin places were so important that the first task of a fifth-century Celtic believer was to find a soul place, or cell, where they could meet with God. These were like prayer closets, which many believers still use today, whether they designate an actual closet or just a special room, porch, or favorite chair.

The Celts also thought that certain geographic formations created a closer place to God. They loved the shorelines, seas, mountains, and cliffs. Each one brought an acknowledgment of God as much as a wedding ring reminds someone of their spouse. I've noticed that many of the places the Celts believed were sacred remain vacation destinations because of their natural beauty and inherent charm. Maybe in our souls we experience an inward pull to certain places for true restoration.

We see examples of such transcendent places in the Bible. For instance, Bethel, Bethlehem, and Calvary stand out as settings for unique spiritual encounters, where the curtain between heaven and earth, the visible and invisible, feels sheer and nearly transparent. Jesus seemed to have had such places that recharged Him and provided spiritual shelter, like the Sea of Galilee, Mary and Martha's house, and Gethsemane. After the Resurrection, the disciples gathered in the Upper Room as they awaited their Master.

I find that certain special places continually draw my attention back to God. Some are local to my neighborhood, others are pockets of the city, and some are outdoors. Some are even in other countries as I experience God's presence in their unique cultural and geographical beauty. Scotland, Italy, Faroe Islands, Iceland, and the Bahamas have become thin places for me where prayer flows easily and worship comes naturally.

These thin places clearly show us boundary points between the temporal and eternal. They provide a connection to the divine Creator and His immense power, beauty, and holiness. When you will seek Him, God has places for you where He will lead you, make you lie down, and restore your soul.

GOD IS IN THE DETAILS

After people and places, we come to things—sacred items that serve as symbols, souvenirs, and reminders of God's presence in our lives. Certainly, the cross and iconic scenes from the Bible have served the church for centuries as visual and sensory reminders of the sacred on earth. Even gestures, such as the popularity of making the sign of the cross on the forehead in the days of the early church, can be another kind of "soul reminder." In medieval times the bones of saints and other holy relics were carried into battle in order to bring victory or were placed in a church to consecrate it. While we don't always know the authenticity of such artifacts, we can agree that certain tangible objects and sensual impressions direct our attention to God and point us toward the next step in our earthly pilgrimage.

Books do it for me.

The smell of coffee does it for me.

The chirp of birds at dawn.

My grandchild's desire to hold my hand.

The details of such encounters draw me into the presence of God and remind me of His glory. My visits to Italy always seem like heaven touching earth. Walking through the streets and into cafés, I'm over-whelmed with the goodness of God. My wife and I once stayed in a bed and breakfast in Tuscany, where they prepared a beautiful, delicious meal for us. The slow, rhythmic nature of Italian dining—eating, drinking, talking, and breaking bread together—is spiritual in nature. Such experiences help me understand why food and meal-times emerge so frequently in the New Testament: water into wine, loaves and fishes, the Last Supper, and breakfast on the beach.

Today, we move so urgently that we often miss what lies before us. We're so busy we become blind to the ruby petals of roses unfold-ing in the garden on the route of our daily commute. We miss the sweet smell of a summer breeze or the feel of nature's textures. I sus-pect for many of us, the place to begin discovering where God wants to take us is looking around at where we are.

God's presence emerges in the details of our lives. His plan for us does as well. When we seek Him in all areas, in all places, at all times, then we realize that He's there leading, guiding, and directing us. We simply have to pay attention.

AN IRISH BLESSING

Learning to plan and obediently staying the course is important if we're to grow closer to God and mature in our faith. But holding plans loosely and recognizing glimpses of God each day throughout our journey is just as essential. Like jazz musicians playing a spon-taneous freeform set, we must be willing to cocreate with God and follow His lead. This ensures that our results will always be so much greater than anything we could plan and accomplish on our own. We work hard and do our part, and we trust God to guide us and do the rest.

Saint Patrick was so concerned about his fifth-century new Irish believers that he set them on an ordered path to correct poor patterns of paganism. He helped them make a plan that would facilitate a connection with God that would then help them blaze their own trails. Shortly after arriving in Ireland, Patrick immediately encouraged new believers to find a prayer cell or sacred place in which they could commune with God. They were to discover a "thin place" where they felt a greater intensity with God, a fuller sense of His presence. It could be a cave or under a tree or even, as many preferred, the edge of a cliff! Anything that invigorated the soul and drew them closer to focus on Him.

Next, Patrick urged them to look for soul friends, like-minded believers who could pray, encourage, and share their pursuit of God in daily life. He knew that community is essential for growth of the soul and wanted Christ-followers there to help one another. These soul friends were not necessarily ahead of them or behind them in terms of spiritual maturity, but simply individuals willing to come alongside them as pilgrims committed to following Jesus.

Patrick shepherded all believers into various small groups for growth and study. He sought for everyone to have a spiritual vocation as they pursued living in their divine purpose and flow. He also challenged believers not to be separated from pre-Christians, wanting them to remain in relationship to some degree with those who did not know Jesus. The influence of the growing communities needed to continue throughout all of Ireland.

Many historians and church scholars believe that, as a result of Patrick's loosely held plan for spiritual growth, more than a hundred thousand people came to know Jesus in a country that had pagan roots, suffered widespread superstition, and lacked major roads connecting villages. Perhaps Patrick knew that what worked in Britain or Europe or Rome or anywhere else in the world was not necessarily what would work in Ireland. Perhaps he trusted that God would meet them there on the Emerald Isle and reveal Himself in ways unique to the place and its people.

We can learn much from Saint Patrick's example, as well as those of many other faithful believers willing to follow a plan and even to go off plan when necessary. This is the divine balance we seek in our own lives, moving toward the goals God sets before us while trusting Him each step of the way. As you plan your life and follow the Spirit, may you experience both freedom and security to accomplish His mighty deeds. Move in the grace of God and begin the journey of being confirmed into a destiny in God. As John prayed for early believers, I bless you with the same: "Beloved, I pray that you may prosper in all things and be in health, just as your soul prospers" (3 John v. 2).

YOUR VIEW FROM HERE

If you don't know where you are going, you'll end up someplace else.

—YOGI BERRA

1. When have you most recently sensed God speaking to you or trying to get your attention in an unexpected way? What message do you believe He wanted to convey? How did you respond to this message? Did it confirm the direction of the plan you were following or cause you to change course?

2. How difficult is it for you to be engaged in the present moment and notice the clues of God's presence? When was the last time you set aside time to unplug and spend time with Him? When will be the next time?

3. Make a list with three columns: People, Places, Things. Take a few minutes and under each one brainstorm

as many responses as possible. In each column, circle one name or item that you want to pursue this week as a way of experiencing God's presence. Your pursuit might be video-chatting with a long-distance soul friend, treating yourself to a bouquet of your favorite flowers, or listening to a special song or piece of music.

"Speak, Lord, for your servant is listening."
—1 Samuel 3:9 NIV

CHAPTER 5

NOT TO SCALE

Sizing Up Your Foundation

If the foundations are destroyed,
What can the righteous do?
—PSALM 11:3 ESV

Our greatest fear should not be of failure but of
succeeding at things in life that don't really matter.
—FRANCIS CHAN

One of the most important aspects of any map is often overlooked: its scale, the ratio used to depict the real landscape in a much smaller form on paper or screen. Most maps include a legend, or key, for interpreting distance—something like one inch equals one hundred miles. If the scale is inaccurate or misrepresented, then the entire map suffers numerous errors and becomes that much harder to use.

From my experience, this problem is similar to having a foundation for your house that's too small or too weak to support the structure you're building. So as you consider how to open your prophetic life map and begin following the path God has for you, it's essential that you consider the foundation of your beliefs, which provides the scale or basis for how you process information and make decisions.

HOW FIRM A FOUNDATION

A proper foundation in Christ makes all the difference in a well-built life. Your foundation establishes the ways and means for how you conduct yourself on planet Earth. It includes your worldview, your general perspective on life, and the filters you use to process information. While it's rarely something we identify and deliberately choose, our core belief systems are shaped by many different variables. We all make choices based on something from somewhere. Those choices weld together a life that can range from consistently chaotic to emphatically beautiful.

Many societal foundations are shaped by the masses and the collective understanding of various groups and individual influencers. There are various voices out there vying for your affection and attention, but only One promises the adventure of a lifetime—for all eternity. The example and teachings of Christ provide a blueprint for how we can build lives worth living.

For followers of Jesus, He is our foundational cornerstone. He is the narrow gate to life. Many terms and metaphors describe the way to true life with Jesus as the foundation. We are instructed by the apostle Paul to "build with care" (1 Cor. 3:10 NIV). The instruction to Christians is to build on a sure foundation, Jesus Christ:

> For no other foundation can anyone lay than that which is laid, which is Jesus Christ. Now if anyone builds on this foundation

with gold, silver, precious stones, wood, hay, straw, each one's work will become clear; for the Day will declare it, because it will be revealed by fire; and the fire will test each one's work, of what sort it is. If anyone's work which he has built on it endures, he will receive a reward. If anyone's work is burned, he will suffer loss; but he himself will be saved, yet so as through fire. (1 Cor. 3:11–15)

The foundation is important as well as the materials used to build. God invites us into a design project that will bear great beauty. Having Jesus at the core is essential. Your personal encounters with Him, your inculcation of His words and teaching, and your daily habits and spiritual practices all contribute to cement a strong foundation impervious to the storms of life and invasions by unexpected events.

KEY INGREDIENTS

Three key building materials go into the supernatural, Jesus-centered, Spirit-forged foundation for your life: absolutes, cultural customs, and personal preferences. Absolutes are established as the strongest part of your foundation. For us as believers, our absolutes are anchored by our unwavering, nonnegotiable beliefs in an everlasting, unchangeable God. In his powerful book called *Thou Shall Prosper*, Rabbi Daniel Lapin stated, "The more that things change, the more we need to depend upon those things that never change. And the timeless truths never do change."[1]

ABSOLUTES

We must have absolutes as part of our foundational view of life and the world as we know it. They provide irrefutable and immovable parameters that serve as a governing guide for how we live. Absolutes anchor our understanding of reality and provide rudders for our choices. No matter how much we might want them to change, true absolutes simply will not shift. Our circumstances fluctuate, our feelings race up and down the spectrum of human emotions, but absolutes remain constant. For example, your body will not grow physically younger. The sun will rise tomorrow morning. Earth's gravity pulls objects to the ground when you drop them.

Just as we have physical and scientific absolutes, we also have spiritual absolutes: God exists outside of time and space as we know those dimensions. He runs the universe and is intimately interested in the affairs of His creation. He sent His only Son, Jesus, in human form to live as a man, die on the cross, overcome death, and pay the price for every person's sin once and for all. If you believe in Jesus Christ and accept the divinely inspired authority of the Bible as God's Word, then these absolutes are clear.

Curiously enough, however, we are in an age in human history when many people deny the existence of absolutes. Perhaps their denial in part results from our tendency to declare personal opinion as absolute facts. For instance, eating hot dogs will kill you. While they may be linked to illness or wreak havoc with your digestive system, not everyone who eats a hot dog will die from it. Not unless they put ketchup on it! I'm joking, but this example makes my point.

People tend to make their subjective experiences and resulting conclusions sound like absolutes in order to intimidate or manipulate the opinions of others. On the dangerous extreme end of this spectrum, we find cults—whether religious, political, social, or cultural—insisting certain rules are absolutes and must be embraced and maintained by all members. They thrive by manipulating members with fear and conformity. "Our way or no way!" they demand.

Fearful of such extremism, especially when it comes to so-called absolutes that tend to meld religious and political beliefs, many people have shied away from accepting any absolute beliefs. Without absolutes in our personal faith, however, it's challenging to know what we truly believe. In many ways, having a firm foundation in Christ frees us to sidestep popular opinions and cultural trends. Instead of shifting with the culture or conforming to the demands of others, we stand strong in the timeless power of the living God.

CULTURAL NORMS

The second component of our spiritual foundations comes from cultural norms and social values. These are strong societal beliefs, often derived from moral or spiritual absolutes, but distinct in their intent to promote and maintain cultural and societal harmony. Establishing a speed limit is an example of this kind of practiced belief. The majority of citizens agree that it would be safer if drivers don't exceed certain speeds in certain conditions. As a result, in busy urban areas with lots of pedestrians, as well as in areas close to schools, parks, and churches, speed limits remain low. On the other hand, speed limits are generally higher on open highways and in rural areas with less traffic.

Curiously enough, in some areas we see that breaking the speed limit becomes a cultural norm. Whether the rationale for the original limit becomes outdated or the majority of drivers have simply decided to ignore it, exceeding the speed limit becomes the norm as more and more people do it over time. Of course, there are also consequences of violating cultural norms, as anyone who's received a speeding ticket lately will attest.

The cultural customs you were raised under will influence your decisions. Many of these are not necessarily laws but simply rules of etiquette or polite social practices. While they're clearly not absolutes, they provide social lubrication for getting along with others and interacting in ways that are respectful and socially acceptable. For example, there's nothing wrong with a natural bodily function such as burping, but doing so on a first date or at a dinner meeting for work may affect how others view you. As long as cultural norms do not violate God's absolutes, most people consider it wise to practice them.

PERSONAL PREFERENCES

The broadest influence on decision-making is your set of personal preferences. What do you like just because you like it? There may or may not be any kind of explanation for your choices other than you simply prefer strawberry ice cream over other flavors or you find that the color green pleases you more than any other. We all gravitate toward items that please us in some way or provide some kind of personal payoff, whether it's something pleasing to our senses or something that engages us because of our temperaments, personalities, or past experiences.

What is your favorite food, TV program, or kind of music? These are all personal preferences and help shape the way you see the world and the decisions you make. Everyone is entitled to these kinds of personal opinions. It's great that I love Italian food and enjoy arguing with friends about why Neapolitan pizza is the absolute best on the planet. But to insist that everyone who disagrees with me is wrong or stupid would be carrying my opinion too far.

Obviously, when a personal preference is asserted as an absolute, problems arise. Some personal opinions—such as generalities about gender, race, ethnicity, and appearance—lead to behavior that's disrespectful, unkind, or harmful to other people. These often emerge out of negative, subjective experiences but can shift to cultural norms if enforced and accepted by others. Consider the way women were not considered worthy of the right to vote or own property for more than a century in our country or the way people of color were legally mistreated for even longer.

Personal preference is the icing on the other two layers of your foundational cake. They are often what others know first about you based on the way you present yourself and the lifestyle you maintain. Privately, your absolutes and cultural norms will guide your life. Publicly, your personal preferences reveal the size, color, and volume of your life. Personal preference should have some say in our choices of life, but they also require thoughtful scrutiny in light of following Jesus and obeying God's commands.

CORE CONVICTIONS

The foundations of homes and buildings are generally unseen and do not invoke the oohs and aahs from visitors like the aboveground structural components. Nevertheless, foundations support everything beautiful above and provide the basis for the ultimate strength of their structure. Unfortunately, the foundations of most buildings erode over time. The forces of nature, impact of inhabitants, and external attacks continually test the quality of the foundation's materials, design, and construction. If the foundation is weak, then it will crumble quickly.

The number one enemy of a foundation in most facilities is water. Usually a life-giving force, water can also be destructive when it permeates the wrong places. Your house foundation can be eroded or destroyed by water in multiple ways. It's important to note that water can be absorbed in ways other than direct contact with the foundation. A soggy roof, clogged gutters, internal leaks, and saturated soil provide multiple points of moisture absorption that can contribute to eroding a house's foundation. Without an adequate drainage system away from the house, especially its perimeter in all directions, water softens the sturdy foundation upon which the structure stands.

Trees planted too close to a foundation can cause root problems that also test your foundation. One of my daughters is a Realtor, and she's seen many houses devastated by root invasion. A tree's roots not only lift the foundation, but they also create a domino effect that often runs through the entire structure of a home, sometimes making it uninhabitable. Improper soil preparation around and under the foundation can result in even more devastating effects. Soil can shift if not packed properly, causing settling that may incur costly bills to re-dig and realign your foundation.

Just as natural foundations of buildings can weaken or suffer compromise, so can our personal foundations. In fact, Jesus emphasized the importance of following His example and obeying His teachings by using this very metaphor:

> Therefore everyone who hears these words of mine and puts them into practice is like a wise man who built his house on the rock. The rain came down, the streams rose, and the winds blew and beat against that house; yet it did not fall, because it had its foundation on the rock. But everyone who hears these words of mine and does not put them into practice is like a foolish man who built his house on sand. The rain came down, the streams rose, and the winds blew and beat against that house, and it fell with a great crash. (Matt. 7:24–27 NIV)

When you anchor your foundation on Christ and in God's truth, you don't have to fear life's storms and the often-tumultuous changes in circumstances. Your life's foundation relies on a God who responds to your cries. When difficulty and torment trickle into your life and threaten your spiritual foundation, He rises up with limitless power and raises a standard against them. This term *standard* is a potential picture of the ultimate standard that was raised at the cross of Jesus Christ. His blood washed away the powers of darkness in eternal ways. Your foundation is ultimately at the feet of Jesus, fully submitted to His great work and the eternal love that covers a multitude of sins. He is the Foundation and stands strong to protect its warranty.

BUILDING MATERIALS

Let's look deeper at the core and quality of your foundation in Christ. What will keep it from destruction? How can you avert future disaster in belief? How can you strengthen and shore up your foundation?

Many of your greatest threats will come to your foundation from those things near you. Destructive influences need to run off and flow away from you like water through a drainpipe. Holding on to habits that are not godly, retaining hurt or bitterness, and ignoring spiritual practices damage your foundation and divert your destiny. When founded on the bedrock of Christ, you can survive a stormy environment without suffering the destructive effects.

So be attentive to what you believe and how you behave. Think about why you act the way you act and make the decisions you make. Be aware of those planted near you. They can deteriorate the foundations of what you believe. Instead, focus on relationships with those who can contribute to a community reinforcing and strengthening your foundation.

Ultimately, your success in life can be determined by epic core choices. The art of building can be traced back to creation, and the use of the term *architecture* can be traced back at least several thousand years. One of the earliest written sources on this topic seems to be *De Architectura* by the Roman architect Vitruvius in the first century AD. According to Vitruvius, a strong, well-composed structure should satisfy three principles: *firmitas*, *utilitas*, and *venustas*—loosely translated as "durability, utility (practicality), and beauty." Like three legs of a stool supporting the seat, these three comprise the qualities working together to support a sound structure. These three also provide helpful categories for assessing our personal foundations.

DURABILITY

Durability speaks to the robust quality that can endure time and weather. Durable materials enable a structure to remain strong and firm for years and years. To create a firm life, materials are important. Paul referred to wood, hay, and stubble as being inferior for a lasting and effective life.

A life that involves longevity of days will also involve choices for correct building materials that strengthen your long-term goals. A successful and fulfilling career is created by information, training, coaching, and strategic preparation. Suffice it to say, you live a life with intention and make recommended choices to shore up the foundation. You practice good stewardship of the resources God entrusts to you.

PRACTICALITY

The second leg of the architectural stool is *utilitas*, or the practical aspect of building. It needs to be reasonable and useful for its intended purpose. Similarly, discovering your unique gifts, talents, and abilities is vitally important to your foundation and how you explore your life's path. Without a purpose bigger than yourself, it's impossible to experience true contentment and personal fulfillment. God created you for a specific mission, one that's ongoing and growing even as you read these words on this page. Your divine purpose in life must be a core part of what you believe and how you align your life with those beliefs.

We each want to build a life that fits our skin. It's so easy in this modern social media culture to live and morph into other people's lives. Your life needs to line up with the absolutes of the kingdom yet be unique to you in God. Your life purpose also needs to pay the bills! Your life needs to function well with and within the culture around you.

Jesus lived a practical life while on a spiritual journey. He had a family and friends, worked a job, and eventually emerged into a ministry with followers. That was a supernaturally natural life. He wasn't religious, just spiritually attuned and focused. He was a human living in an ancient Hebrew culture overruled by a Roman culture. He was subject to multiple authorities, not the democratic constructs we presently enjoy in our nation.

Christ's life was very practical. He kept His eyes on Jerusalem but still functioned in this realm. He understood the tension of being a spiritual person in an unspiritual world. "We are His workmanship, created in Christ Jesus for good works, which God prepared beforehand that we should walk in them" (Eph. 2:10). We are experiencing our great inheritance in Christ while learning to practically walk it out in everyday life.

We live as beings born again with new life from above in an earthly realm with brokenness and imperfection. We are created from above to shine as a people who know how to navigate life. We do not stand out as culturally weird but as a transcendent attraction to an alternative life on earth. We pay our bills. We mow our lawns. We shop at stores. We are not weird just for the sake of standing out. Our practical living becomes a message of the favor of our God.

BEAUTY

Finally, architectural beauty speaks to how aesthetically pleasing a structure is to the eye. While the criteria for a beautiful building has shifted over the centuries, along with tastes, trends, and technology, the appearance of a home, office, school, or store has a huge impact on the way people respond and use the space. Beauty is often the most noticed and least appreciated of the three qualities.

During times of economic depression or severe limitation, aesthetics are often compromised or eliminated. Unfortunately, we can also fall into this trap when we experience calamity or crisis in our lives. But God created us to look for beauty and to share it as a reflection of His character and creativity. As we focus on durability and practicality of life, we must not neglect beauty.

Several years ago I read a book by Brian Zahnd called *Beauty Will Save the World*. In the prelude of this lovely book, Brian shares the story of the medieval Prince Vladimir the Great of Kiev. Apparently, Vlad was looking for a new religion for Russia and sent out envoys to investigate some key religions and report back.

While they found some of the religions "dour and austere," their investigation of Christianity in Constantinople stunned them. "They led us to a place where they worship their God," Vlad's scouts reported, "and we knew not whether we were in heaven or earth, for on earth there is no such vision nor beauty, and we do not know how to describe it; we only know that God dwells among men. We cannot forget that beauty."[2] The Russians adopted Christianity because of the beauty they found celebrated. True beauty always feeds the soul.

You are a builder of something beautiful. You are a temple of God's Spirit, an ambassador of Christ, and a child of our heavenly Father. The life that is intended in Christ for you is a life that lets you experience heaven on earth. It will never be perfect on this side of heaven, but as the psalmist said, you can "taste and see that the LORD is good" (Ps. 34:8 NIV)!

Assess your foundation with honesty and objectivity. Invite the Holy Spirit to inspect your life's foundation and to show you how to make it even stronger and firmer. Consult with the Author and Finisher of your faith and see what areas need shoring up, or even replacing. If your foundation is crumbling in some spots, then do what's required to strengthen it in ways that will sustain you for the rest of your life. God is in the business of restoration and renovation, so let Him complete His good work in your life. By following the example of Christ and being empowered by His Spirit, you can build a firm, practical, beautiful life!

YOUR VIEW FROM HERE

You can't build a great building on a weak foundation.

—GORDON B. HINCKLEY

1. How would you describe the foundation at the core of who you are? Are the choices that you make day to day carrying you into stability and strength? Is your life a life that you love? Does it support your life purpose? Does it serve your dreams well?

2. How is your life durable, practical, and beautiful? How can you apply this criteria to your career, marriage, family, and church life? How is beauty a part of your foundational beliefs?

3. After spending a few minutes in prayer asking the Holy Spirit to guide you, grab a notebook or journal and inspect your life's foundation. Focus on the categories we explored in this chapter by identifying your absolutes, cultural norms, and personal preferences. Then assess the ways your current life foundation is durable, practical, and beautiful. What grade or evaluation would you give in each of those areas? Which one seems the strongest? Which one needs the most attention for improvement?

As you come to him, the living Stone—rejected by humans but chosen by God and precious to him—you also, like living stones, are being built into a spiritual house to be a holy priesthood, offering spiritual sacrifices acceptable to God through Jesus Christ.
—1 PETER 2:4–5 NIV

CHAPTER 6

WAYPOINTS

Encountering God Along the Way

Draw near to God and He will draw near to you.
—James 4:8

We are designed as a resting place for the Spirit
of God, changing every environment that we
walk into.

—Bill Johnson

On any journey, using any map, you inevitably discover places
that exceed what you expected. These may be historic sites that
stir your patriotism, quirky attractions you find by spontaneously
taking a detour, or vistas of unrivaled natural beauty. They may also
include the people you were with, the season or weather during your
visit, and the unique experience you enjoyed there. In many ways,
these waypoints provide the color, flavor, and texture of your journey.

For instance, I can't recall my last trip to Italy without smiling at the thought of the exquisite hand-rolled pasta my wife and I enjoyed at a small, family-owned trattoria. Watching the honey-gold sun melt into the rolling hills of Tuscany, tasting the fresh herbs in our food, and listening to the soft music of a violin from across the courtyard—these and many other details became a time and place that touched me deeply. I had no choice but to praise God and enjoy the blessings He was pouring out on us that evening. This singular experience blended into an unforgettable event that colored our entire trip.

Such experiences are not just for road trips and dream vacations. On our spiritual journeys, God wants to manifest Himself to us and show us the sites of His kingdom. In order to enjoy them fully, however, we must have an open heart to connect with Him. We need to pay attention and become attuned to His Spirit. These waypoints, encounters with God on our journey, can propel us into our destiny and reveal more of where He's taking us and what He has in store for us.

Waypoints offer us glimpses of God we might miss if we're not paying attention, experiences that heighten our senses in ways that make us feel fully alive, and revelations that point us in new directions on our journey of faith.

DREAMS

Waypoints are not only places but experiences that draw us closer to God. Last year, I had an early morning dream. Filled with many details, the overall feel of this complex dream centered on heaven, almost as if heaven were a person in a particularly good mood! It sounds crazy, I know, but there was no mistaking that this dream was significant.

When I woke up around 5:30 a.m., my dream lingered, and I sensed the presence of Jesus in a strong, palpable way. So I asked God if He would allow me to continue my dream if I went back to sleep, and internally I heard Him say, *Just close your eyes.* I've learned over the years that God is often much more practical than we realize. Of course, I needed to close my eyes if I expected to doze back into my dream. Closing my eyes as instructed, I instantly received revelation and understanding about each of my four children.

God clearly had something to share with me. Flowing fast and furious through my mind, this message became so intense that I reached for my phone while still lying in bed and began to write down everything the Lord was sharing. The experience overwhelmed me, and I began to laugh—not in the usual way we laugh at a joke or a friend's anecdote. No, my laughter was like an automatic expression of exhilarating joy! As I sensed God's good mood and brushed against heaven's edges, I felt euphoric.

Fully immersed, I asked the Lord to take me deeper without losing my mind.

He did!

The flow continued for three hours. Words flowed as fast as I could write—over my kids, their spouses, and their children. It was magnificent. At some point my wife woke up, probably due to my laughter, and asked what I was doing. I began to read her my notes. The Spirit of God in the room was thick, like a pulsating wave of cleansing liberation. As I read, laughter bubbled from inside me yet again.

My extreme joy became contagious then, and she joined me in a wild fit of laughter. Trying to speak through my soul's giddiness, I explained that I hadn't gone insane but had come close! As she got up to go prepare breakfast, I savored the taste of heaven lingering with me. After a three-hour encounter with God, I didn't want this awe-inspiring experience to end and wondered if it was confined to my bed.

I got up and went into the shower to prepare for the day. As the water beat down on my head, I felt God's presence come close again. He spoke to my heart and said, *I will give you everything you want that rhymes with* old *in the alphabet.* Weird, right? But in the moment, I didn't question it. The feeling was the joy of playing a game with my parents when I was young. My heavenly Dad was offering me something, so why question it? Later, I would recall the verse expressing God's desire to give us good gifts: "If you then, being evil, know how to give good gifts to your children, how much more will your Father who is in heaven give good things to those who ask Him!" (Matt. 7:11).

If anything, it was funny that God used the term *old*, because I had referred to it so often in the past two months after my birthday. There was a sense that He had been listening to my lighthearted complaints about my advancing age and was in on the joke with me! I absolutely loved this. My Father's casual but powerful humor was reassuring to me and rocketed my trust.

While showering, I began to go through the alphabet, letter by letter. I came up with eight words that rhymed with old: *bold, cold, fold, gold, hold, mold, sold,* and *told.* The Lord then spoke and said that each of my children was marked by one of these words, and instantly I knew which one was for each of my children.

Getting on with my day, I kept returning to this incredible encounter and God's divine revelation. What did this mean? In the days that followed, I felt His residual presence clinging to me, like glitter confetti after a party or a favorite scent that lingers long after the flowers have faded. Always bubbling beneath the surface, this encounter gave me keys for understanding more about my children and God's promises for their lives—and mine. I began to feel as if I had been given a relational road map for each of them. Those three special hours with God helped me understand them and the new families they were now beginning with their spouses. God had reset my views of them and infused me with hope. What a great gift of grace!

Even as I was sleeping that night, God prepared me for a transformation.

In my most restful moments of the day, He opened heaven's doors to unlock mysteries of my life. While I could have easily passed off that encounter as a remnant of a wild dream or the pizza I ate the night before, I've learned to pay attention and receive what God wants to give me. God is pragmatic when it comes to giving us clues about our destinies.

That waypoint changed my perception and clarified my views. That encounter lingered for days, infusing me with energy, joy, peace, and a carefree lightness—and that waypoint continues to resonate with me to this day. Without a doubt, I know God in a closer, more intimate way now.

LANDMARKS AND MILESTONES

In every journey, there are always waypoints: those stops and cross-roads where you take note of where you are and where you're going, the places where you pause and take in the view. They may be as quick and refreshing as a deep breath and drink of cold water or last for hours, days, or longer and include a variety of sensual details. Spiritual waypoints are similar to the sites, events, and experiences on a travel itinerary.

The other day, my wife and I were looking through pictures from a recent vacation. When we couldn't remember the name of the bed-and-breakfast where we stayed, I pulled up the app I had used on that trip. Opening the map still marked with our routes, we saw both our intended travel plans as well as the places we ended up going.

Every waypoint contained a memory. Although each one looked like a squiggly line or dot on a map, it told a story. I remembered why we took certain turns and how our minds changed as we continued the journey. Some became much-needed places of rest, while others surprised us with unexpected delights. They were also key places of decision-making for the remainder of our trip. They were the landmarks and milestone moments of our trip.

At a waypoint, you're often checking the map and looking ahead. Am I on the correct road? Do I have what I need for the next leg of the trip? Are there new skills or provisions that are needed? Have I lost sight of where I'm going?

Similarly, spiritual waypoints offer places to rest as well as intersections where unexpected encounters—with other people, events, or situations—often occur. They allow us to listen more closely to what God wants to say to us and to readjust our direction accordingly. They move us closer to our goal of being conformed to the image of Christ as we gain momentum toward heaven.

CLOSE ENCOUNTERS

We see many people encountering God at waypoints in Scripture. Jacob found a spot called Luz that he renamed "Bethel," which became a turning point in his path. Jonah found himself in a whale's belly, an experience that literally expelled him into obedience to God. Content to herd sheep in the wilderness, Moses discovered a burning bush had a different plan for his future.

Jesus Himself stayed in a desert for forty days to experience time alone with His Father without interruption. Christ knew He would need this encounter to nourish and fuel the public ministry He would soon launch. Jesus demonstrated how energizing it can be to come out of a wilderness waypoint in the power of God's Spirit.

These waypoints are meant to be places of remembrance and refreshment on the arduous path of following Christ. Our waypoint encounters propel us, refuel us, and make necessary course corrections.

They usher us closer to God and move us forward into His light. They reveal Jesus to us and allow us to see who He is and how He is at work in our lives. These waypoints become clues on our trek through uncertain times and dangerous passages. Through spiritual moments of divine connection, we know who we are and where we're going. Jesus restores our sense of direction as the ultimate True North by which we each set our soul's compass. We see Him in nature, hear Him in culture, find Him in Scripture, and sense Him in worship.

Encounters with Christ change everything and restore our vision.

These waypoint moments produce micro-awakenings within you. For a brief period, they allow you to see new possibilities or a different direction. If you were drifting prior to pausing at a waypoint, then you shift and get back on track for your true journey. If you're already on the right path, you get affirmation or confirmation regarding your destiny. These encounters with Jesus provide the best road signs marking the narrow path as you follow in His footsteps. I love the way this passage from Scripture explains these spiritual milestones:

> Nevertheless when one turns to the Lord, the veil is taken away. Now the Lord is the Spirit; and where the Spirit of the Lord is, there is liberty. But we all, with unveiled face, beholding as in a mirror the glory of the Lord, are being transformed into the same image from glory to glory, just as by the Spirit of the Lord. (2 Cor. 3:16–18)

Several things happen when you encounter Jesus. When you turn to the Lord, a greater liberty comes upon you. This turning is the essence of repentance, which is simply no longer going your own direction and instead moving toward God. Whether encounters lead to full U-turns or just slight course adjustments, they continue to free you but also expand your potential.

We're continually moving from darkness to light in this life. Even someone who has received Jesus is still on this earthly, mortal, temporal side of heaven. We're in a spiritual battle, but our victory is assured as we follow Him. From waypoint to waypoint, our encounters with Jesus transform us and shape us from glory to glory. Each new connection with Christ moves us closer to Him, while being transformed into His very image.

PILGRIMAGE OR PARALYSIS

Waypoints are essential for advancement on our journeys of faith.

They are also places where we can get stuck. Whether it's a literal geographic location, a certain mind-set, a powerful relationship, or an ego-appealing career role, these waypoints eventually become snares that prevent us from moving forward. In more than forty years of coaching and counseling people, I've witnessed many people who come up to a dream fulfillment only to shrink back. It might be the fear of success or the fear of failure, shame and guilt or anxiety and depression, but they become paralyzed and can't cross over into the promised land they've worked so hard to reach.

The energy to keep going evaporates, and what was intended as a waypoint becomes a permanent stop. Our pilgrimage becomes paralyzed by too many possibilities we don't want to face. We lose sight of God and the sound of His voice in our lives. We flounder and drift even as we become more restless and untethered. Our lives' narratives no longer seem to have meaning, purpose, and passion.

I recently heard a quote attributed to John Barth that speaks to this: "Everyone is necessarily the hero of their own life story." With this in mind, I'm convinced a healthy person will adjust their memories to serve them a better history. They will see God's hand at work in their lives even when they're still struggling and waiting on healing, restoration, and redemption. This kind of hope is a survival mechanism that God gives us. It keeps us from deep grief and regret. Our minds search for a reason to make us heroes.

Even as our minds search for reasons to make us the heroes of our own stories, we can also become our greatest antagonists. Depression and despair can pervert the story you tell yourself and cause you to become the villain in your own story. This change of thinking can truncate your spiritual journey and leave you wandering in the wilderness.

You choose to be a victim or a victor. You stop and get stuck because you doubt your own ability to move on. You create a waypoint that becomes a prison, a temporary pause that becomes a lifetime of paralysis.

DON'T STOP NOW

So many people get stuck in a good thing that was meant to be temporary. College is a great example of this. Inevitably, you can find a group of perpetual students who never graduate but remain in their college towns. They become stuck in the temporary and often unrealistic environment of college life. As paralyzed students, they may not want to leave friends or the memories they've created. They won't risk the present for a future that might mean new geography, friends, and challenges.

Too often, we get stuck wearing a Band-Aid when all has been healed. We get stuck in immature and uninformed theology that holds us in place. Views of the gospel that include legalism, exclude women in leadership, and depict a God without power will limit your advancement and strand you in a quagmire of fear and doubt. Trauma can also become a waypoint that stunts your spiritual growth. A diagnosis, a failing relationship, a surprise attack on your finances or family—any one of these can get you focused on yourself and away from your spiritual path. But you don't have to remain stuck.

God has greater power to free you than you can imagine.

How then do we move on with what God has called us to do? How do we keep from getting satisfied with the status quo? If we're stuck or have drifted off course, there is always a way forward through the power of God's Spirit. There is never a reason to stay in a place that is not moving you toward the life you believe God has for you. You should never settle for less than God's best for your life. When you encounter Him, you encounter His life and His dream. You become energized and clarity returns.

An encounter with God provides an invitation to continue on your journey.

OUT OF THIS WORLD

I became a Christian when I was eight years old. Our family attended a Baptist church, and one summer in 1965, a visiting hell-fire preacher sparked my future path as I decided to follow Jesus. We continued to attend that church, but at that church a grand encounter with God was usually only reserved for a salvation experience. My mother, though, was a bit of a mystic. She knew things that happened without empirical evidence. She would hide herself in a closet and pray for many hours, and I became accustomed to her cries of desperation to a loving God. She was a woman of first-hand encounters with God.

Everything changed for me when my mother began attending a Pentecostal church. I was soon dragged to the same church against my desires. This new church was much livelier. Suddenly, my mother was like a fish in water, and her prophetic insight swam to new depths in this cultural environment. She often became a bit ecstatic, seeing and hearing things from God at an increased rate. You can imagine how difficult it was being a teenager with a mother who had access to supernatural powers and insight!

But her world has now become my world too. Early on, I began to experience great, powerful encounters of weeping, laughing, and speaking in unknown languages. That became my norm and began to mark my life. Soon, I became expectant of ongoing encounters with God. Listening for Him to speak, I anticipated His verification of my considerations and decisions. I entered a life of encountering Him on a regular basis.

I believe in this kind of relationship with God. His Word says, "My sheep listen to my voice; I know them, and they follow me" (John 10:27 NIV). We should expect to hear from God and connect with Him. In our prayer times and Bible studies, in our small-group meetings and church services, we should come expecting an encounter with the living God. He wants us to know Him and to be changed by our knowing.

We see this kind of life-transforming encounter in the Transfiguration: the encounter Peter, James, and John had on a mountain with Jesus, Moses, and Elijah (Matt. 17:1–9). Undoubtedly, that encounter stirred the three disciples deeply. Peter's first desire was to build three tabernacles (v. 4), which is not surprising because God's presence makes us want to do something.

Even when you hear what God is asking you to do, don't leave the encounter too quickly because of your enthusiasm. God often is after something deeper. We see this as God interrupting Peter's enthusiasm with this exhortation: "This is My beloved Son, in whom I am well pleased. Hear Him!" (v. 5). They all fell on their faces until Jesus came and helped them up. Peter left that encounter with an adjusted understanding of whom he was serving. He also saw this waypoint of his journey as an education and not a habitation. He didn't build the tabernacles but carried on with the Lord's plan.

Encounters with God and glimpses of heaven will change your

trajectory. Encounter-filled waypoints serve as a reminder of who God is, who you are, and what you are called to be. These reminders break us out of normal, sometimes passive behavior and into hope again. A lifelong culture of encountering God will always point us back to Him. Moses was hiding in the desert until he encountered a burning bush. Gideon was hiding from his enemies until the angel of the Lord appeared. Peter was an ordinary fisherman until Jesus walked by. If you keep encountering God in worship and Scripture and life itself, then you will be always moving toward the purposes of God.

HEAVENLY BREAD CRUMBS

Even when you find a waypoint, not everyone responds properly to an encounter with God. We can easily see it as an anomaly or a one-off experience. We read of famous people who have an encounter with God, but without proper framework, little fruit and no lasting change emerges. Encounters are like invitations from heaven. They are a gift to open a window, walk through a door, or answer a call on your life. The impact can fade away, however, if a framework is not built to sustain the moment of change. An encounter with God may not include a promise, only an invitation.

God always reveals Himself in your life. He shows up, you behold the moment, and you are changed. Your life's trail is marked by God's bread crumbs. The prophetic life you live is one that includes moments and seasons with God. These are not just feel-good seasons but energizing visitations for ultimate habitation. In these encounters, you learn of Jesus and become like Him. You review your journey and look at next steps. You listen closely and look for the signs God has left for the turn up ahead. His Word promises that if we seek Him, He will draw near to us (James 4:8).

Learn to be present, soak in the moment, and create a resting place in God.

Encounter His presence along the journey of your life.

Be empowered by His Spirit and transformed by His love.

Look for the next waypoint—God is already there!

YOUR VIEW FROM HERE

It is wonderful what miracles God works in wills that are utterly surrendered to Him.
—HANNAH WHITALL SMITH

1. What experiences come to mind when you consider the waypoints on your spiritual journey? What were the circumstances? How did God speak to you or reveal Himself in these encounters? How have they changed you and forged a stronger relationship with Him?

2. When have you gotten stuck or lingered too long at a waypoint? What prevented you from going forward? Why were you stuck? Think about the various emotions you felt during that time of being stuck and list them. How did you finally break free and start moving again? What did you learn about God from this experience?

3. Spend a few minutes in prayer seeking God's presence. Then grab your journal or a notebook or create a new document on your tablet or laptop. Think back on the most recent waypoint encounter you've enjoyed in which you sensed God speaking to you about your life. What specific message did He share regarding your

health, your family, your career, your ministry, or some other aspect of your life? How did you respond? How does His revelation continue to resonate in your life today?

Whether you turn to the right or to the left, your ears will hear a voice behind you, saying, "This is the way; walk in it."

—Isaiah 30:21 NIV

CHAPTER 7

YOUR PROPHETIC PASSPORT

Honing Your Personality for the Long Haul

Keep your heart with all diligence,
For out of it spring the issues of life.
—PROVERBS 4:23

The heart is the mainspring.
—SMITH WIGGLESWORTH

Several years ago, while driving through Indiana, I saw a sign with my name on it—literally! Advertising a local pub, it read: "Tuesday Nights, Karaoke with Steve Witt." Really? Not only was there another Steve Witt in this world, but he was known for doing karaoke! I considered going to the show just to support my double but instead kept rolling toward my destination. Later, though, I did search online to see just how many Steve Witts there are in the world.

As it turned out, there's a soccer star in Australia, a country-western singer, and an unusual variety of teachers, coaches, and trainers all with my same name. Looking at the age ranges and various demographics, I was struck by the contrast among all of us sharing the same name but living such vastly different lives. Since that discovery, I've actually befriended several Steve Witts over the years via social media. One of them is a pastor from another state, whom I occasionally lift up in prayer. I often wonder if he and I and the fraternity of other Steve Witts share any other qualities in common—like singing karaoke!

NATURE AND NURTURE

Perhaps you've had a similar experience. But no matter how many people share my name or yours, the uniqueness of who we are typically emerges in our distinct personalities. Like snowflakes and fingerprints, each one of us is different from any other human being. In fact, our uniqueness can become our prophetic passport to new and greater possibilities. But what accounts for our intrinsically unique personalities?

Philosophers, among others, have been debating answers to this question for more than twenty-five hundred years. Their responses fundamentally come down to nature or nurture or some combination of both. Are we born with our personalities innately hardwired into our DNA? Or are we shaped and molded by our families, environment, social systems, and culture? And if it's both, which seems most likely, what's the percentage ratio for who we end up becoming?

Obviously, there's likely no definitive answer. While certain aspects of a person are inherited genetically, our personalities are also affected by geography, circumstances, and environment. Trauma can impede or truncate growth of a person emotionally and psychologically. Similarly, positive opportunities and advantages can enlarge or uncover hidden aspects of who you are, facets that might otherwise remain undiscovered or in the distant background.

Over the years, I've become quite a student of human nature, and I'm continually impressed by the complexity and creativity of so many unique personalities. Life's challenges can often cause one person to harden and another to soften. While personality profiles can provide insight, they're often limited by the shifting variables affecting people. For instance, you may be very outgoing at work, yet more reserved at home. You may come out of your shell in a crowd of friends, yet clam up in a small group of strangers. Personalities shift in the sands of environment and the winds of culture.

That is all the more reason it's important for you to look at your own personality and the variables, good and bad, shaping who you are and where you're going. Any assessment has limitations, yet I've also witnessed the enlightening power they wield to help a person become more aware of themselves and their place in the world around them.

While we are all different as we experience life directly filtered through our individual personalities, I have to believe that we are hardwired with certain propensities, yet shaped through environments and love itself. Atmospheres can calm, invigorate, and incite shaping outcomes of a personality. Parents can have huge influence on their children by creating boundaries measured in love, joy, and peace.

Most people begin their lives interpreting other people based on comparisons to their own perspective. It's easy to use yourself as true north when you're probably the person you know the most about. From that self-focused starting point, it is usually easy to interpret diversity as negative. The differences of others may seem frightening, dangerous, or intimidating. Therefore, the thought that other people need to be more like us is not surprising. We then try to conform people to how we see ourselves, which creates tension and resistance.

Somewhere along the way, however, usually in school or in marriage or at work, we understand that differences can be enlightening, enjoyable, and exciting. We eventually lay down judgmental weapons and celebrate diversity of personality. We realize how boring it would be if everyone were just alike. I've worked for decades in coaching and training using personality profiles and seeing the dynamics of how they affect a person's success. The biggest inescapable lesson learned from these profiles is that we are all different! It is a necessary process in growth to acknowledge others and accept them as they are and to realize the benefit of the differences.

DISC JOCKEY

I always liked the DISC profile for its simplicity. As one of the primary assessment tools, it provides a broad-stroke look at human differences. From my experience, it's the gold standard of personality profiling, both a great starting point and recurring reference point as you pursue learning more about yourself in relation to your life.

In the DISC system, personalities are broken down into four major categories: Dominance, Influence, Steadiness, and Conscientiousness, creating the acronym DISC. While you can find many DISC assessments online with more detailed information, let's briefly consider each of these four personality types.

DOMINANCE

Ds, the first type, are dominant directors with a passion for results. They tend to get things done quickly but not always cleanly.

They're achievers who "git 'r done" and move on. They see the big picture, leap to bottom-line conclusions, and can get frustrated with long meetings or slow action.

INFLUENCE

The *I*s are influencers. They're people oriented and in many cases can be the life of the party, placing a high value on fun. They can turn a boring meeting into an unforgettable event. Some of my favorite people are *I*s. Although fun to have around, they can sometimes take their eye off the ball and fail to follow through to completion. They are less purpose oriented and more energized by people. If you need to recruit people or develop a lively presentation, they may be a good source.

STEADINESS

The *S*s are steady and social, particularly with small-group or one-on-one type connections. You can usually spot them at a party: they're the people standing in a corner somewhere talking with one person with deep concern and continued affirmation on their face. *S*s are deep lovers of people and will invest time and money to build relationships. They're gems and make up the majority of almost any population group.

CONSCIENTIOUSNESS

The *C*s are cautious and conscientious. They're naturally motivated toward detail and perfection. They suffer much criticism for being sticklers of the law who follow the rules and always making sure things are done right. They help keep people and organizations in line and out of jail. To them being on time is important as well as sticking to the agenda. They are the quality-control people who remain steadfast in their resolve. You always want a *C* on your team to help provide structure for goals and to transform dreams into reality.

All these personalities have positive and negative attributes, and none of us is perfectly aligned with any one of these categories. We're blends of many personalities. In fact, I'm a *D-I*, which means I have a fast personality. I'm a quick decision maker, love to include groups of people, and have fun in the process. Under pressure, though, I can become autocratic.

Sometimes we have different nuanced personality expressions, depending on our geography, social group, or personal circumstances. My experience shows that a wounded *D* can at times act like an *S*, or an abused *S* can become very demanding. None of us fits perfectly into any single category all the time. We're all different, like bank safes that have ever-changing combinations. We can never crack the code in a way that is permanent and definitive. Our growth often occurs in the process of changing the combination from day to day. Without ever solving all the secrets of our human personality, we can still enjoy discovering new dimensions to other people and discern different aspects of ourselves in the process.

HEAVEN COMES DOWN

While we know we are new creatures in Christ, a new creation, according to the Bible (2 Cor. 5:17), does becoming a Christian change our personality? There's no direct evidence of this in Scripture that I can find. While we change and become more like Jesus, we also seem to become more authentically who God created us to be.

We can definitely see this maturity in the life of the apostle Peter. In his time with Jesus, he seemed to slowly move toward a Christ-centered life. Peter was known for his directness, which could occasionally cause problems, yet it still seemed intact on the day of Pentecost. His impulsive personality appeared to shift from judging people or cutting off an antagonist's ear to taking a bold stand and lifting his voice to preach (Acts 2:14). Peter continued to grow and become more a man of wisdom, including writing two epistles of the New Testament. But he was still Peter—passionate, smart, caring.

Peter is not the only example of God using a person's personality for His divine purposes. While you might feel intimidated if your personality is more subdued, in the Bible we often see low-key underdogs become giant-slayers and kingdom builders. Elisha, David, Moses, and Abraham all began as shepherds who grew in wealth, position, and authority. As they followed the Lord and experienced heaven's power, they grew in greatness. Their personalities remained the same but caught on fire. They did great miracles, defeated giants, led millions, and started a family that became a nation outnumbering the stars of the sky! Otherwise humble, quiet, solitary people can become dynamic leaders.

You have an earthly or temporal personality and were thrust into the world with a born propensity toward whatever you inherited from your parents and ancestors. Your home life may have caused you to gravitate toward or react against traits such as neatness, anger, humor, or pessimism. You are a conglomeration of all your experiences, and your personality is the product of decades of personal, sometimes unintentional, crafting.

Without strong biblical evidence, we are sometimes confined to understanding our earthly personalities and not so much the effect of heaven on them. The philosopher and theologian Augustine saw the City of God descending and impacting the City of Man. Heaven comes down and touches the human experience. You begin to change for the good, conformed into the image of Jesus, as you crucify the flesh and its deeds. This is the battle of overcoming the fringe and fallen aspects of your personality in order to reflect your identity in Christ.

But this is definitely a work in progress. A while ago I heard about a Christian woman who was confronted by a coworker who chastised, "I thought you called yourself a Christian!" She quipped back, "I said I was a Christian—I didn't say I was Christ!" Our lives are always being pruned and nourished by the Holy Spirit and God's Word to shape and fashion us into stronger, more godly men and women.

KEEP THE CHANGE

The Bible doesn't directly address personality, but it is clear that the various characters are motivated and respond diversely. Jacob's sons became the twelve tribes of Israel. In Old Testament times there was some degree of proactive recognition of traits in a human. We see it demonstrated in the naming of Jewish children. In some cases it was out of frustration, in others it might have been from observation, while still others were named by a desired or prophesied destiny.

A quick glance at Genesis 29–30 gives us a field of personalities from the children of Jacob with an array of unusual names that later became identified with their eventual tribe. Judah means "praise" and indicates a tribe of warring musicians that will emerge. Simeon's name means "heard," which indicates a thanksgiving to God. Some of the children's names reflect what the mother was going through at the time, such as the name Gad, meaning "fortune has come," or Asher, meaning "happy." The blessing of Jacob on his sons in Genesis 49 goes into further details of emerging personalities. These blessings shaped the futures of his children.

Even those born into questionable circumstances and given dubious names could grow into a tribe of people renowned for their integrity. For example, Issachar seems to have been born under questionable intentions, which was reflected in his name, meaning "hired man." Not exactly a vote of confidence from your father!

Later, Issachar was called a "strong donkey" but without the negative connotation lacking courage or being disloyal. Eventually, the tribes of Issachar became strong warriors fighting for Deborah as well as early supporters of David as king. Finally, they emerged as sages who understood the times and knew what to do (1 Chron. 12:32).

Your personality can shift with the realignment of your soul. In other words, your character can affect your personality. Your commitment to Christ changes you!

FOUR FACES

While it's hard to consider God as having a personality in the way we experience them, we are created in His image as His children. And we certainly see a variety of facets and dimensions within the Trinity. The Holy Spirit is seen like a dove yet also comes in like a mighty wind. Jesus loves the little children yet turns over the tables in the temple. God the Father is loving enough to send His Son, Jesus, to die for us but emerges as punitive at times in the Old Testament regarding His dealings with humankind.

Regardless of the various aspects of the Godhead, it seems clear that our personalities can be refined and purified by our encounters with the Lord. We see this in 2 Corinthians with a kind of presence transformation. Can our personalities be touched and pruned in His worshipful presence? Do our corporate Sunday services do more than we think? Is our worship God's way of changing us and empowering us with heaven's attributes? What happens when you begin to behold the face of the Lord? We're told, "We all, with unveiled face, beholding as in a mirror the glory of the Lord, are being transformed into the same image from glory to glory, just as by the Spirit of the Lord" (2 Cor. 3:18).

We are clearly changed in the presence of God. In Ezekiel we're given a stunning look at the interiors of God's presence. The creatures around the throne have been there a long time, worshipping. With four faces and four wings, they're described as mobile, moving, all-seeing creatures. They do not turn when they move and have wings with eyes all over them. These are creatures of His presence: "Wherever the spirit wanted to go, they went, because there the spirit went; and the wheels were lifted together with them, for the spirit of the living creatures was in the wheels" (Ezek. 1:20). I wonder if this is what it looks like when you stay in the presence of God. They are living examples of what happens with long-term exposure to the Son!

If we're being shaped into a person of His presence, then I suspect our personalities are being influenced as well. Each creature's four faces resemble a man, a lion, an ox, and an eagle. They look as if they're natural in origin but obviously take it to the next level in some kind of supernatural hybrid.

HUMAN

The human face is above all other faces in this passage and represents wisdom, initiative, innovation, and design. We know what to do when the Spirit needs us. As one of the faces of God's presence, we create things like our great Creator. We make decisions and rise above the entire natural kingdom with prowess and ingenuity.

Our spiritual self also moves quickly with wings of speed and eyes looking to the past and the future. We see above and beneath. We are fully aware of what is around us, and our goal is to move where the Spirit is going. We are circumspect. But it doesn't stop there.

LION

The lion is royalty and boldness. Regardless of your earthly temperament, out of the presence of the Spirit even the quietest, most reserved people can roar. We're told in Scripture that "the wicked flee when no one pursues, but the righteous are bold as a lion," (Prov. 28:1). Now, that's authority! God can touch a worshipping personality and infuse boldness when it is needed. We worship the Lord because He is great, but we come out of it changed by His fragrance and the Spirit's empowerment. When you spend time close to God, you can expect a radical increase in your boldness over time. That is what happens to creatures in His presence.

OX

Next, the face of the ox represents the strength of the burden bearer. This is the serving, suffering face of obedience to the Lord. No struggle will crush us. We can bear them all and still take more. God's presence brings us strength. Scripture tells us that "much increase comes by the strength of an ox" (Prov. 14:4). The ox is the worker producing one of the revenue streams for the kingdom of God, and as such its presence will increase your strength and cause your sphere to grow. Energy to do and become flows from the presence of God. Jesus was led into the wilderness yet came out in the power of the Spirit.

EAGLE

Finally, the fourth face is that of the eagle. Now a key symbol of our nation, we can easily imagine the soaring eagle in all its glory. Above the fray with the ability to see movement for up to two miles away, eagles can dive at speeds up to two hundred miles per hour! Rather than getting caught in the shortsightedness of a temporal life, this bird soars above it. This is its nature. Similarly, when we're in God's presence, we can rise above the limitations of our circumstances and all we see around us. We cannot be contained by earthly cages. The Bible proclaims, "Where the Spirit of the Lord is, there is liberty" (2 Cor. 3:17). We have been set free!

Many have speculated that these four faces represent the four Gospels and the distinct description of Christ that each provides. Some believe that Luke shows Jesus as a man, Matthew as a lion, Mark as an ox, and John as an eagle. These variations may indeed represent the personality of God through Jesus Christ. Jesus was a Man of great wisdom, the Man sent from God the Father. He was the Lion of the tribe of Judah, the Burden Bearer, and the mighty Eagle. He is the One we are emulating as we are transformed into His likeness.

FACE THE TRUTH

Don't get discouraged by your limited view of your personality or by the assumption that if you haven't changed certain aspects of who you are by now that you'll never change. All things are possible through God! I have a good friend named Jerry who's a great leader with a good heart, but he'd always felt some type of internal limitation in how he shared love.

Then at age fifty-one, Jerry experienced God's presence at a conference where the Holy Spirit recalibrated his very soul. I watched it happen! The guest speaker called Jerry up onto the platform and took him through an activation that had stunning effects. Afterward, tears flowed easily as Jerry's heart was opened and expanded. He says that the transformation has been so advanced that it almost feels like he was born again! Love now flows freely through Jerry, and his worship is unrestricted.

Don't get stuck in a box of misunderstanding your personality. Some people will want to pigeonhole you. But regardless of what earthly limitations you might have, you are by no means limited. Your personality is important, but it is meant to position you on earth. If you understand yourself, you will begin to know how to position yourself. Take some personality profiles and figure yourself out. Allow the Lord to mold your character and your personality. Let the presence of heaven shape you into the faces of heaven. You can become the force of heaven in an earthly personality!

Imagine a personality of whatever type being impacted by heaven. Christ being formed in you can dramatically change your odds for success here on earth. More importantly, you will be fashioned into a person who worships freely, soars over mountains of grief and fear, and boldly speaks clarity and wisdom during times of confusion. You have enormous capabilities when affected by the presence of God.

Jesus modeled this full spiritual maturation on earth. He was the God-man. The Word made flesh. Jesus was shaped by the human touch and godly instruction for thirty years in preparation for His three-year period of public ministry. He remains Emmanuel, God with us, and we're still looking at His magnificent life as our example!

THE GARDEN CREDO

Considering Christ as our model of personality perfection, let's look briefly at some of those silent shaping years prior to His public ministry. The Bible is intentionally vague on His upbringing, leaving only a few verses to reveal His maturation. Perhaps the best known summarizes considerable growth in several key areas: "Jesus increased in wisdom and stature, and in favor with God and men" (Luke 2:52).

Sometimes to understand the pieces of a puzzle, you need to see that larger picture. Based on what we see throughout the Bible, Jesus' personality is expressed in five core mandates that, if remembered, would serve us well regardless of temporal influences. They are first revealed in the garden of Eden and culminate in the Garden of Gethsemane. Your alignment with these aspects of Christ's development can slowly change how you present yourself in what you know to be your personality.

In the beginning, God created the first garden as a place anchored by choice for His human creations. Adam and Eve could eat the fruit from the Tree of Life or the fruit from the Tree of Knowledge of Good and Evil. This decision was ever before them. As they soon found out after making the wrong choice and disobeying God, the environment beyond Eden was quite different. Within the garden, however, we glimpse aspects of God's personality that illuminate our understanding of our own. There we find a set of God-shaping mandates, or credos, first established in the garden of Eden.

These truths are important to God and, therefore, will be important for you and me as well.

This chart demonstrates the expanding garden or kingdom to which God calls us. These five credos give us a look into what was important to God in the garden and likewise is still important to Him now. Based on these, we can respond to His desires and spread God's fragrance of love. If you align your life to these core understandings, you can create a life that mimics and becomes a garden life.

If these were important to God from the beginning, then it stands to reason He hasn't changed. This is the way God is. It's His personality. God is still manifesting these credos through His kingdom. Our lives push from the center out, expanding the garden of the Lord to all the earth. These should be key beliefs, vital for each of us. That is how it was in the beginning, and it's how it is now. This is the personality of God!

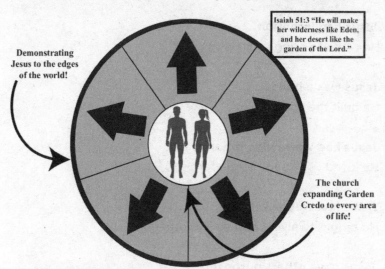

GARDEN CREDO

The following chart illustrates the 5 aspects of the Garden Credo that when activated expand the influence of God into every area of life. The expanded garden effect even in deserts

Isaiah 51:3 "He will make her wilderness like Eden, and her desert like the garden of the Lord."

Demonstrating Jesus to the edges of the world!

The church expanding Garden Credo to every area of life!

1. **Tend and Keep** - An inward desire to align with God's purpose by caring for what is given to you in yourself, others, and your surroundings. **Tend your garden**.
2. **Not Good to be Alone** - Focusing on community and relationships in order to reveal the creativity and power of multiplication. **Embrace relationship**.
3. **Walk with God in cool of the day** - Form Spirit-breathed ritual in daily encounters and worship with God. **Walk with God**.
4. **Be Fruitful and Multiply** - Seeking out results in all you do. Bearing fruit for others to benefit from. **Multiply stuff**.
5. **Fill, Subdue, and Rule**- Become assertive and wise in expanding the influence of the King and His kingdom. Seek to serve in problem solving and vision casting. **Expand God's influence**.

CREDO:
a statement of the beliefs or aims that guide someone's actions.

JESUS' PERFECT PERSONALITY

Someone once said, "Jesus is perfect theology." I love that! He is God in the flesh. Do you want to know what God would do and how He would act? Then study Jesus. He fulfilled all the above mandates in His lifetime. Here are just a few of my takeaways from studying Jesus' perfect personality:

Jesus had intention.
He came to bring us life abundant.

Jesus was a builder.
He built the church.

Jesus had worldwide dreams.
He loved us enough to die for us.

Jesus invested in eternity.
He taught twelve disciples and others.

Jesus gave others purpose.
He sent His followers into the world.

Jesus loved children.
He cherished and protected them.

Jesus did miracles.
He went about doing good and healing all who were oppressed.

Jesus resisted dead religion.
He condemned legalism by religious hypocrites.

Christ lived a life that was both ordinary and extraordinary. His ministry extended from His personality. He set the standard we continue to follow today. Following Jesus affects your personality. Day by day, you're being conformed into the image of Christ. Regardless of your earthly, temporal personality, you will change as you grow closer to Him and find your identity in Him. His thoughts, His actions, and His influence will shape your personality and transform your destiny.

If you want to live to the fullest, then commit your personality to God. You will still be unique in your personal texture, color, and shape, but you will also be transformed by His loving touch. Your personality is key to the beauty of life. God created your personality, and you can use it to grow and expand your relationship with Him. After all, He is the Potter and you are the clay. You are His workmanship created for the cause of heaven!

YOUR VIEW FROM HERE

Love is the only way to grasp another human being in the innermost core of his personality.
—VICTOR FRANKL

1. How would you describe your personality? What three words best describe who you really are? What would those people closest to you—family, friends, coworkers—say about your personality? Has your personality changed over the course of your life or basically remained the same? What evidence do you have to support your answer?
2. What personality tests, profiles, and assessments have you taken? DISC? Myers-Briggs? Enneagram? CliftonStrengths? Something else? How accurate do

you consider the results of past personality assessments you've done? In what ways have they helped
you most?

3. Spend some time in prayer and ask God's Spirit to help
you see your personality fully surrendered to Christ.
Then take some time to think about areas in your life
that you would like to see conform more to the image
of Jesus. Write these down in a notebook or your journal. Consider how you can allow God to use the full
extent of how He made you for His purposes.

For we are His workmanship, created in Christ Jesus
for good works, which God prepared beforehand that
we should walk in them.

—EPHESIANS 2:10

CHAPTER 8

BORDERS AND BOUNDARIES

Making Prophetic Decisions Your Default

See, I have set the land before you; go in and
possess the land which the Lord swore to your
fathers.

—DEUTERONOMY 1:8

First I make choices. Then my choices make me.

—ANDY ANDREWS

Living a prophetic life involves making a myriad of choices. The
Bible begins with Adam and Eve choosing between life or death,
and it ends with Jesus knocking at the door of our hearts, forcing
us to choose whether we will let Him in. Throughout the pages
of Scripture, we see how God's gift of free will requires us to take
responsibility for the decisions we make in life. Learning how to make

good choices is essential in our obedience to God's Word and dealing with our day-to-day challenges.

GOOD UNDERSTANDING

By the time we're adults, most of us have developed a default way of making decisions. In order to see your life more prophetically, however, you must look through the lens of heaven. The voice of the Lord is so important in making decisions.

When I step away from my emotions and wait on the Lord, my mind clears. Consequently, I review the prophetic words over my life on a regular basis and look for similar themes among them. Some are voice recorded, and some are written down. Some of them are major words, and some are minor words. Prophetic words come in different sizes, just like decisions.

Some major decisions need closer attention and time. This is especially true with major life events, such as marriage, relocation, career, and so forth. Minor ones include the rudimentary movements of an average day, such as what to wear, whether to eat cereal or yogurt for breakfast, when to schedule a dental appointment, and so on. Smaller decisions often shape the way you make larger ones, so it's good to think about how you make the choices you don't usually think about.

Most importantly, though, as you examine the way you make crucial choices in life, you must seek God's presence and listen for His voice. Pay attention to the prophetic words over your life. The apostle Paul wrote, "This charge I commit to you, son Timothy, according to the prophecies previously made concerning you, that by them you may wage the good warfare" (1 Tim. 1:18). Use prophetic words as weapons and tools for your future. Learn to hear God in them and respond.

Often I have made major decisions based on prophetic words. My response time is based on many things. Much of it is how the word made me feel. Did it shake my bones? Did it rock my world? Did it confirm a path that God had been laying out for me for some time? Even then, I pause and wait for confirmation. Our best choices are linked to good understanding. Revelation from God can bring that good understanding. Good understanding helps us discern the God-direction of our lives.

THE FIVE R'S

Most of us are conditioned to respond to life's challenges in three ways—reactive, robotic, and reflective. In addition, we need to also consider a fourth and fifth: responsive and revelatory. Here's a simple way to compare them:

> **Reactive:** impulse with emotion
> **Robotic:** automatic decision without thought or process
> **Reflective:** thoughtful consideration before action
> **Responsive:** changing held ideas gently over time
> **Revelatory:** radical shifting in awareness based on epiphany

REACTIVE

The first two are dangerous. Reacting with raw emotion can cause considerable damage. Many people have developed a life pattern of responding in this manner due to fear. But fear-based reactions can end in bankruptcy of relationships, finances, and resources.

ROBOTIC

Robotic decisions may work occasionally in some situations but do not account for the anomalies of life that need clear thought and strategic action. You need to be present mentally and emotionally in major decisions. Robotic, or automatic, decisions tend to be uncontrolled, effortless, fast, unconscious, and skilled. In other words, you have a history of success in these types of decisions that allow you to move quickly and freely.

REFLECTIVE

Reflective decisions, on the other hand, are controlled, effortful, deductive, slow, and rule following. These are the ones that take time and reflection. Both decision-making processes require wisdom, but each uses it in a different way. Reflective decisions are usually the best kind when left to our own devices. Researching and pausing yield wisdom, especially for major decisions. Unfortunately, this method tends to be earthbound—we're limited by what we find on Google or watch on YouTube.

RESPONSIVE

I've noticed in charismatic Christian circles a tendency to exalt the automatic-response decisions. For some reason they just feel more Spirit-led. However, I've found that this decision-making process can end with dire consequences if generally applied. When you hear a prophetic word or have an experience, the feeling is so strong that you might jump to an automatic decision. I've seen people quit good jobs, sell a house, or even marry a person because of a word they applied as automatic.

I've also witnessed people make painstakingly slow-response decisions that should be automatic. The life experience of the individual should erupt with wisdom, putting minor decisions in their proper place. Some decisions don't require deep dives or divine direction, but our most important decisions do.

REVELATORY

These last two methods, responsive and revelatory, transcend our human rationale, logic, and instinct. They draw on information contained in heaven. They allow you to seek God's wisdom in ways that are revelatory and prophetic. The Spirit's guidance changes everything. When followed faithfully and obediently, you can receive insight on every major decision and many daily ones.

Responsive and revelatory decisions are meant to be part of every Spirit-filled believer's life. They're influenced by prayer and God's Word, along with books, sermons, songs, art, conversations, and natural events that speak radically to the soul. Local churches need to equip the saints in proper interpretation and application of these mysterious heavenly insights. One requires immediate change and response, while the other is a spiritual discipline for the long game.

PROPHETIC RESPONSES

My approach here is to help you major on the majors and minor on the minors. When making decisions, learn to recognize what is automatic and move on it quickly. A minor decision has little consequence. This is a practice area for moving in heavenly wisdom in an earthly realm.

Major decisions must be met with a strategy, filled with hearing the voice of the Lord. The counsel of trusted friends and family and the recognition of proper preparations can help also. Take the time, use your spirit and your mind, and you will build a long-term success.

Check out my Prophetic Response Chart (next page).[1] I created this chart a few years back for my own use as a practical way to assess prophetic words over my life as well as a guide for major decision-making. The risk lines measure level of risk that is self-determined but should be discussed with friends or mentors. The bottom horizontal line measures your response. This response is an inner feeling that best comes from soaking in the Word of God and daily relationship with the Holy Spirit. Explanations of each quadrant and how to respond are written below the chart. The goal in every major decision is to lower the risk if possible and to raise the response of faith.

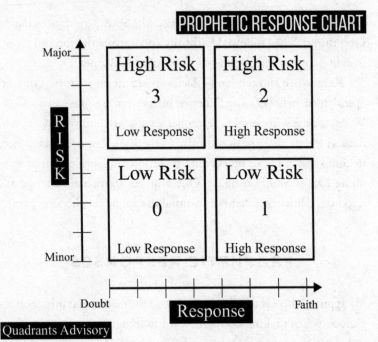

PROPHETIC RESPONSE CHART

	High Risk 3 Low Response	High Risk 2 High Response
	Low Risk 0 Low Response	Low Risk 1 High Response

Major — Minor (RISK axis, vertical)

Doubt — Faith (Response axis, horizontal)

Quadrants Advisory

0 = Low Risk/Low Response. These are everyday decisions. What you eat for breakfast. What color socks you wear. Learn wisdom to not be frozen by small challenges. Make a choice! If God gives you a prophetic word that involves low risk and low response, I doubt that it demands a response at all. Just move forward smartly! Is it even a word from God?

1 = Low Risk/High Response. If this chart was color coded, this would be green for "go." You have high faith for it and it is low risk so you are good to go. If a barrier is in your way, remove it or rebuke it, but don't let it stop you. In this quadrant, you have godly wisdom and confidence that it fits with your plan. Always move with prayer and circumspection, but move. Confirmation is helpful, but not essential. Maintain your faith with the Word of God.

2 = High Risk/High Response. The quadrant would be colored yellow for caution. You have high faith for it, but it is high risk. The upper half of the chart deals with major life decisions like purchase of a house, choosing a spouse, partnering in business, etc. I recommend spiritual counsel from someone you trust, reading the Word of God for revelation, and get numerous confirmations. As your understanding regarding risk increases, then your sense of risk decreases. Faith grows and perception of risk shrinks. This will drop the choice into box 1 making it easier to deal with.

3 = High Risk/Low Response. This quadrant would be colored red. This is a game stopper. If you are facing a major life decision and you are low in faith, do not proceed forward. Gideon and Moses asked for confirmations, you should also. This is where a fleece is appropriate in my opinion. Get spiritual counsel. You may even want to put the decision on the shelf until faith grows, moving it to box #2. Fasting is appropriate whenever you are puzzled but especially in box 3. Fasting increases your sensitivity to hearing God, therefor bringing greater clarity. If a barrier is up in this box, it is not the Devil, it is God stopping you! Explore the choice, but do not move forward until your risk drops or your faith increases.

DOOM LOOPS

In his bestselling book *Good to Great*, Jim Collins talks about a decision-making process that creates a "doom loop."[2] According to Collins, a doom loop or death spiral can occur when you start making decisions based on emotion rather than thoughtful analysis. He illustrates how disappointing results can lead to reaction without understanding. That reaction can trigger new direction, leader, or fad to hastily try to correct a downturn. In other words, one bad decision can beget another, triggering the downward spiral. Poor direction then can lead to no buildup, accumulation, or momentum, which yields more disappointing results, and the spiral continues. Such cycles often result in personal or corporate failure, even destruction.

Collins lists signs of a doom loop that include seeking breakthrough rather than buildup, using hyperbolic communication to create momentum, refusing to face facts, and leaving a pattern of chronically inconsistent choices. I recognized these errors in my own life and would encourage the prophetic community to review them. We're all guilty from time to time of trying to create something in a hurry rather than doing the good work of building it over time.

BOOM LOOPS

If our reactions and poor decisions can result in more reactions and worse choices, I've often wondered if the opposite is true. If something can go downward in a spiral of bad decisions, then why can't good decisions drive you upward? Wise, prophetic decision-making should pave the way for more of the same. When we listen to God and follow His Spirit, we learn to rely on Him more and more. Borrowing from Collins, this is what I call a "boom loop."

Boom loops grow by consistently making wise decisions. I love the practical, yet dynamically spiritual, decisions made in the book of Acts. We see in Acts 2, when the Holy Spirit fell upon them, the followers of Jesus moved with what happened. Peter took his stand and preached, with astonishing results. That is prophetic leadership at its best. He responded to the movement of God and quickly adapted to the practical challenge of hosting long-term guests. Order seemed to emerge quickly as they routinely devoted themselves to doctrine, fellowship, breaking of bread, and prayer. As a result, we see a seminal thread of seeking and responding was sewn into the new community.

Growth always creates new challenges. In Acts 6, a complaint arose against the Hebraic Jews for their bias against Greek-speaking Jewish widows. They respond immediately with wisdom and administration, giving direction to appoint leaders that are "full of the Holy Spirit and wisdom" (v. 3) to be given to this business. That allowed the apostles to continue in prayer and ministry of the Word, thus balancing practical structures and spiritual insight.

Wise, Spirit-led decisions created peace then just as they create peace for us today.

SPIRIT IN ACTION

I have found an alarming trend toward extremes in many churches today. They are either business oriented and heavily structured with an emphasis on measurable results, or they're intuitively led with fluid structures that aren't sustainable. The New Testament, however, shows us a blend of the two. Referencing Jacob's dream, with angels descending and climbing a ladder between heaven and earth (Gen. 28:10–19), the early church created the same kind of bridge. With prayers going up and God's solutions and provisions coming down, we see the ascending and descending of messengers once again.

This dependency on bridging heaven and earth emerges later in another decision we see in Acts. A visiting prophet named Agabus was shown by the Spirit that a famine was coming to the land (Acts 11:27–30). In this early church, we see such a reverence for the prophetic that the apostles responded with an offering before the famine was ever evidenced. How far have we drifted from that willingness to hear and obey God?

We also see a prayer meeting going on while Peter was delivered from jail. When Peter tried to get into the meeting, the people praying were hesitant to believe it was him, thinking it must be his angel (Acts 12:12–16). Once again, we see more evidence of organizational structures interceding with amazing spiritual results.

In Acts 13, the leaders of Antioch were ministering to the Lord when the Holy Spirit spoke. It was a directive to separate Barnabas and Saul for a missionary work. They responded accordingly with fasting, prayer, and the laying on of hands to send them away. This is prophetic decision-making, a heavenly blend of Spirit and action. This kind of leadership directs decision-making into the arena of God's presence to produce refreshing and highly effective results.

This is what the boom loop is all about, discernment that rises from time spent with the Lord. It's listening for a word from heaven and then acting on the wisdom of Scripture to bring practical results that bless the community. It is an ever-increasing clarity and precision of choice that helps avert disaster. This ascending loop can create a culture of continual successful decision-making: a spirituality that depends on heaven but moves with efficiency, not hiding behind a "waiting to hear from God" delay.

Boom-loop leaders can be quick to respond or refer matters to more prayer and discussion. They know we're called to seek the Lord but also to move on what He says. Sometimes it will be moving on what has already been said. This is wisdom. Boom-loop decision makers don't rely on exaggeration or manipulation to sway a crowd. They don't push decisions through quickly to avoid embarrassment. They're willing to face facts, yet strategically pray their way through them or appoint spiritual people to solve them.

They know that facing facts is not a lack of faith—just the opposite. Wisdom from God empowers a culture of people who know how to solve problems. God has an answer for everything if we learn to hear from Him. Prophetic leaders don't fear the response of those they serve, and therefore they don't try to appease everyone or solicit popular opinion. They know that the momentum of their church community does not rely on them but on God's Spirit. When aligned with the Spirit, the pace of rhythm of your movement is naturally determined.

Follow this decision-making process and you may find that you are ascending into a movement of the Spirit that may touch the world. It will not be perfect, but it will be less stressful and more fruitful. We need to learn from one another, but not at the expense of avoiding our own exercise of discipline before God. We must focus on response versus reaction: a reasonable process of seeking and a wise course of loving application. Good decisions beget more good decisions. If you develop the skill of wise decision-making, you will excel and opportunities will come to you. The mistakes in the garden of Eden created a sinful doom loop, but the obedience of Jesus Christ created a redemptive boom loop.

LEAN TOWARD THE LIGHT

Plants almost always grow in the direction of the sun or their source of light. We grow in much the same way. It's always important to lean forward in the direction where God is leading us. The Lord takes "no pleasure in the one who shrinks back" (Heb. 10:38 NIV). We're told, "Without faith it is impossible to please God" (11:6 NIV). So we lean into life, willing to risk by stepping out in faith. Rather than linger in your own uncertainty, you lean into the *yes* of God. Yielding your gifts and passions to God opens gates of opportunity.

Many opportunities may come naturally through friends and family, but they can also be created. Surrendering our currencies and passion in simple service can inadvertently open spiritual portals. Jesus said to "give, and it will be given to you" (Luke 6:38 NIV). Isaiah says, "If you extend your soul to the hungry . . . then your light shall dawn in the darkness" (58:10). There's a correlation between serving and giving of self and the reward of connection. Opportunities tend to show up when you consistently step out in faith and obediently follow God's Word and trust His Spirit.

For example, Barnabas started out as an encourager in the church. His actual name was Joseph, but his great gift of encouraging earned him the nickname of "Barnabas," which means "son of encouragement." His gifts of encouragement and faithfulness opened major gates.

This process is one that we can experience as well. In business, products and services often go through a multiphase process before reaching the marketplace. A new offering begins as an idea and ends with a successful launch reaching the intended target audience. Similarly, we must go through stages and walk through various seasons before we connect with the opportunities we seek. These stages of development are often where you learn and solve issues pertaining to what's needed up ahead. Before you can enter a new phase of the process, you pass through a gate that almost always requires a decision and a direction.

As Barnabas served the emerging community, opportunities opened. He went from an unknown giver to a friend of the apostles to ultimately an apostle himself. When the new radical convert named Saul came to Jerusalem, everyone was afraid and suspicious of him. Barnabas, however, took a risk and introduced him to other Christ-followers. Once again, Barnabas stepped up, giving what he had to open a door for Saul, who himself was going through a major portal into the most important phase of his life by serving Christ as the apostle Paul.

This action of giving served Barnabas well in the future. He was then sent by the apostles to oversee the emerging movement in the city of Antioch. He assessed the movement and realized he needed help. He went to recruit Paul, who then came and worked with him for a year. Barnabas basically took Paul under his wing, taking risks, giving of himself. He moved from stage to stage by making key decisions that were selfless but undeniably advanced his role in God's plan.

Barnabas and Paul then became a missionary team. Eventually, the anointing of Paul was so strong that the team became known as Paul and Barnabas. This reversal of roles did not seem to be a problem for Barnabas. He continued in ministry, and church tradition reports him as a martyr years later, giving the ultimate gift of his life before entering into the gates of heaven.

PEACE BEGETS PEACE

Opportunities are like planets. They come in different sizes, shapes, and frequency, orbiting in cycles that leave us looking for them to appear. Sometimes we can't see them and assume they're nowhere to be found. Knowing that they will eventually reveal themselves again, however, we must do the only thing we can do in the meantime: prepare! These are the moments when you upgrade and consolidate, looking ahead at your next strategic step. The iconic investor Warren Buffett once said, "When the market is dropping, I am buying." Spiritually, we would do well to follow this advice.

Your difficult or lull times often hold life-altering opportunities. When you feel low, then you should buy into the promise of the summit you're about to reach. Walking in faith requires an investment in what God is about to do. During times of uncertainty or challenge, you can still practice good stewardship of all He's entrusted to your care. You can add to your knowledge, spend more time in the Word, and fellowship with your family. You can expand laterally to learn new fields and pursue new friendships.

I know this firsthand because battling cancer gave me an incredible opportunity. I do not believe that my cancer came from God, nor would I have ordered it, but it changed my mind about moving into the future. I determined not to waste time. I learned aloneness and silence. I came out on the other side with a fresh fervor that remains contagious. I listened more, talked less, and mined other people's thoughts and experiences. Consequently, the most difficult time in my life became a turning point, an opportunity for advancement rather than a crushing crisis.

The prophet Jeremiah, held captive in a foreign land, was also in a place without opportunity. He became unpopular because he realized it would be a lifetime before the people of Israel would get their freedom again. With this awareness front and center, Jeremiah tried to help others engage with the present moment and create their own opportunities for growth and development.

Jeremiah delivered a word from God that was not easily received because it sounded like only more delay, pain, and suffering. God's message for them was basically to keep on keeping on. Like the famous British public service message of World War II proclaimed, sometimes the best course of action is to "keep calm and carry on!"

Jeremiah told them to build houses and dwell in them, plant gardens, and eat the fruit, get married, and have children. Basically, they needed to live life in the present rather than make action contingent on future conditions and expectations. They wanted deliverance right away, but what they got was a lot of time. We're often the same way. We pray for the big breakthrough, yearn for a quick escape, and devise the perfect plan for advancement. But our deliverance often occurs over a lifetime and in the day-to-day operations we faithfully execute. Too often, we underestimate the power of normalcy and faithfulness.

SKY'S THE LIMIT

Jeremiah reminds us of several powerful truths. We're told our constant mission in the midst of low-opportunity moments requires "that you may be increased there, and not diminished" (Jer. 29:6). We forget that it's God's intent to prosper us even in difficult times. Whether it's a bad marriage, frustrating job, false accusation, or serious illness, there is still an increase promised to you. Micro-opportunities lie within your macro-persecution. Potential growth frequently lies just below the surface of disappointment. Never let your life lie in ruins while you are waiting for divine intervention.

Like Jeremiah and the people of Israel, we're told to seek peace and pray for the city of our captivity to have peace. Why? Because "in its peace you will have peace" (v. 7). This sounds counterintuitive. Aren't our enemies the problem? Aren't life's problems blocking our way forward? How can we pray for our captors to have peace? Shouldn't we be praying for them to be punished and held accountable?

Jeremiah releases the key to unlock potential bitterness, self-pity, and hate: Our peace is hidden in their peace. We pray for political leaders we neither like nor agree with. We pray for bosses and companies that exploit our labor. We pray for spouses who don't seem to realize what we need the most. Instead of complaining, quitting, or despairing, we serve these moments with joy.

We trust God in the long game!

After Jeremiah shared God's message of our peace being tied to praying for others' peace in the midst of pain, He then revealed the reasoning behind this instruction. It's one of the best-known verses in the Bible and a mainstay on refrigerator magnets and social media: "For I know the thoughts that I think toward you, says the Lord, thoughts of peace and not of evil, to give you a future and a hope" (v. 11).

Even in our most difficult times, our hope is in the Lord. Our hope is in His future for us and with us. If opportunities are like planets, then lift up your head to the sky. They might be eclipsed by darkness right now, but soon you will see their light!

YOUR VIEW FROM HERE

In any moment of decision, the best thing you can do is the right thing, the next best thing is the wrong thing, and the worst thing you can do is nothing.
—THEODORE ROOSEVELT

1. Describe the way you typically make important decisions. Which of the five types—reactive, robotic, reflective, responsive, or revelatory—best summarizes your usual approach? How has this worked for you so far? What would you like your default method of discernment to be?

2. How does prayer influence the way you make decisions? How does the Bible? What verses or passages has God used lately to speak to your heart? How can you involve God more directly in the way you make decisions?

3. Spend a few minutes in prayer seeking God's presence. Then, grab a notebook or journal and think about your history with making important decisions. Describe the way you usually go about trying to make a big decision, and list some past outcomes of this method. With this in mind, surrender your decision-making to God. Write down a plan for practicing your

own boom loop. How can you use small victories and daily decisions to transform the way you view opportunities in your life?

We can make our plans, but the LORD determines our steps.

—PROVERBS 16:9 GNT

CHAPTER 9

NATURAL WONDERS

Using Temporary Resources for Eternal Purposes

And my speech and my preaching were not
with persuasive words of human wisdom, but in
demonstration of the Spirit and of power.
—1 CORINTHIANS 2:4

The devil fears hearts on fire with the love of God.
—SAINT CATHERINE OF SIENA

Everyone is looking for a special advantage or unique way to improve their life today. We all want insider information or a privileged connection that will propel our dreams forward. We're hoping for something that will touch and transform us, enrich and boost us beyond our normal means. We want something extraordinary to set us apart and enhance our ability to enjoy life. In short, we want life's "secret sauce."

I'm not sure who invented this phrase, but it's made its way into the cultural mainstream and has been part of the business arena for some years. You would suspect it must have come out of the food industry as a marketing lure for some proprietary ingredient that set some brand's food apart from others. Allegedly, in fact, the "secret sauce" phrase emerged out of McDonald's creation of the Big Mac hamburger. Secret or special sauce was meant to separate it from its competitors, adding a distinctive flavor as well as advertising mystique. Now, anything that excels, succeeds, or transcends expectations raises the question, What's the secret sauce?

A KISS FROM HEAVEN

If Christianity has a secret sauce, it is the Holy Spirit's anointing. When you receive God's anointing on your life, its power enhances your potential and fulfills His promises for your life. God's anointing changes the way you look at life and how you proceed on your journey of faith. As it transforms your limitations into God's limitless power, the Spirit's anointing becomes your secret sauce, adding flavor to everything you encounter.

The result is an intensified awareness that creates energy to understand and to receive, setting it apart from all other natural experiences. With an invisible yet very real effect, anointing permeates the air around you like a fine fragrance. It effectively supercharges whoever it encounters and whatever it touches and creates a substantial lift from natural to supernatural.

The touch of God transforms you in character and empowers you with spiritual tools. The Spirit's anointing is essential in crafting a prophetic life map. I have been in rooms when the anointing has come. It was palpable and sparked my world with electricity. Like a kiss from heaven, you know when you've been touched by God's presence.

GREAT EXPECTATIONS

I remember my first visit to the Toronto Airport Christian Fellowship, then known as the Airport Vineyard and famous for its revivals. It was 1994, and I had just returned from a sustained ten-week sabbatical granted to me from my eastern Canadian church. Enjoying the time to recharge my spiritual batteries, I had spent weeks in the United States with my family, studying and being refreshed.

While on this trip, I first heard of the outpouring of God's presence in a relatively small Toronto church, one I knew of but that wasn't connected to any of the leaders in my acquaintance. My sabbatical had been given to me for refreshment, but my soul yearned for something from God that was beyond a physical rest. Intent on experiencing something unique, I committed to visit this church as soon as I returned to Canada.

As I enjoyed my sabbatical, my personal hunger for more began to torture me, especially knowing I'd have to wait another couple of months until I could visit this church in Toronto. Little did I know that it would be a life-altering visit, leaving me with something like a spiritual tattoo, something supernatural that would mark me in a permanent way.

Weeks passed, and I finally returned home and arranged to go to Toronto with some friends. We arrived on a cold Canadian night to a warehouse at the end of an airport runway. It was industrial and rather nondescript, not what you would imagine a revival hotspot to be. Nonetheless, crowds of hungry people had already lined up to get into the church, knowing that space was limited.

Upon entering the building, people began to race to save their seats with their Bibles. I'm not sure I had ever seen such eagerness to attend a church service, yet there they were, moving quicker than I had ever witnessed at my own services. As my friends followed, I quickly reserved several seats in the back and waited for the meeting to start.

The worship band began with songs that leaned into a happier theme. Many people were already worshipping at an intense spiritual level, appearing as if they were drunk or unusually happy. This didn't bother me, in that I was raised in a Pentecostal church and thought I had seen everything with respect to human emotion. Seeing everyone's exuberant worship, I honestly thought that some other Pentecostals had heard about this church and had come to exhibit their spiritual culture.

As a pastor I couldn't help but assess the meeting, and I honestly didn't see what the big deal was regarding their church service. The service was above average, but not reaching the fanatical pitch that I had expected because of its growing reputation. But my expectations were about to be exceeded.

"MORE, LORD!"

Following the worship through music, a kindly bear of a man named John Arnott stood up to speak. He interviewed several people who had obviously been touched by these nightly meetings that had been continuing for three months by then. Healings, dynamic joy, freedom from afflictions, and supernatural peace were commonly repeated among those interviewed. Each of them seemed strangely touched by their experience. Honestly, they appeared drunk! Their laughter was over the top, and their interviewer's questions couldn't squelch the joy overflowing from those people whom God had anointed.

I wasn't skeptical at all, but I figured they were outliers, knowing that dramatic movement by God's Spirit often attracts individuals seeking an elevated emotional experience. Up until that point, I was experiencing nothing unusual. I had no idea what exactly was going on in the invisible, spiritual realm. I was clueless as to the depth of what God was doing even as I was also deeply hungry for more of God.

John preached and then moved into a ministry time. When he

announced this, he invited people to come to the front for prayer. Suddenly, as he spoke over the crowd, he waved his large hand and said, "Come, Holy Spirit!" Immediately there was a rush of an invisible presence as a tangible vibe filled the air. It was as if a tsunami of love surged across the room. Forgive me if this sounds over the top, but it was truly indescribable. It was neither imagination nor hype; it was like God walking into the room.

Many in attendance were falling and laughing all around me. I had seen that before in small doses, but never on this mass level. People all around me were falling into chairs and crashing into one another. I began trying to help them to prevent anyone from getting hurt as their spiritual frenzy only increased.

A middle-aged woman came up to me then and asked what I was doing. She encouraged our team to go up front for prayer. Heading that direction, we quickly saw there was no room left at the front. Bodies were joyously strewn across the floor, and the place literally seemed out of control.

My team had to be escorted over a crowd of bodies on the floor, into an adjoining overflow room. Ministry leaders lined us up for prayer, and I actually anticipated someone touching me firmly on the forehead, causing me to fall down. Instead, I was surprised as a woman held my hand and said, "More, Lord!" Her tone and demeanor made it obvious that this church was not trying to create hype or stir the crowd, but simply to make room for the Holy Spirit to do what He wanted.

UNVEILING THE FUTURE

Then "more" hit me! I immediately felt the touch of God, the anointing. This was definitely the special sauce! My body hit the floor like a sack of potatoes as I was overcome with an atmosphere of joy. I began laughing in such a forceful way that it was as if I was vomiting joy! I know that sounds oddly inappropriate, but it perfectly describes what I was experiencing. Periodically, I would look over at my team lying on the floor, laughing hysterically as well. Those young men, whom I had known for several years, were experiencing exactly what I was. We couldn't move, or maybe we didn't want to. Either way, God was marking our lives.

The Holy Spirit came in waves. More than an hour later, we required assistance and were helped off the floor. When I have told this story to people, they will often ask, "Why did you fall on the floor?" I have come to respond by saying, "Because I could not stand. God's power and joy were so compelling and overwhelming!"

In three days of visiting Toronto, I ended up on the floor, laughing, nine times. I was thoroughly drenched in the Holy Spirit. I had never felt that level of joy for a sustained period in my entire life. Oddly, the next day when I got up, my facial and stomach muscles ached as if I had completed a rigorous workout. Sharing this feeling, I joked with others that I was using muscles I hadn't used in years.

Over the next five years, I was propelled around the world just to share what I had experienced. I witnessed that anointing being transferred to thousands in at least twenty-five nations. My experiences in Toronto have shaped my entire future. That encounter changed my view of God. I could enjoy Him more! It also removed my fear and has left ramifications that continue to hit me until this day. I'm not sure whether my future was changed in those moments in Toronto like a train changing tracks, or whether it was simply unveiled.

SATURATED BY THE SPIRIT

Does God want to surprise us with His continued unveiling of a deeper life in God? Does He desire to take us deeper, from glory to glory, faith to faith, and strength to strength? Paul explained, "Eye has not seen, nor ear heard, nor have entered into the heart of man the things which God has prepared for those who love Him. But God has revealed them to us through His Spirit. For the Spirit searches all things, yes, the deep things of God" (1 Cor. 2:9–10).

I couldn't escape it anymore, nor did I want to. This was my life in God's anointing. My experience along with so many others is not isolated. You, too, can receive this gift and live in the fullness of joy, peace, purpose, and passion that God intends. It is an adventure in the Holy Spirit, constantly anticipating the things that have been prepared by God for each one of us. Committed to a life in the Spirit, you become saturated with His holy Word and enveloped in understanding from the Spirit.

One touch from the Good Shepherd can change all you think and see. After my anointing, I continually rejoice in my salvation and think of Jesus all the time. He is my life. While I knew Him before Toronto and had experienced Him often over the years, meeting Him there and being overwhelmed by His Spirit was different. That meeting was personal and dynamic. It was a Pentecost that went from my heart to my mind and back. That experience was an anointing of God.

You don't have to go to Toronto or anywhere else to experience God's Spirit that way, although there is something to proximity. You simply have to be willing to invite His presence to infuse your life. You simply have to be willing to receive Him.

SHEPHERD'S ANOINTING

The word *anointing* means literally "to rub." Like many terms used in the Bible, it is not strictly a religious term, but a cultural one. In ancient times, shepherding was a common occupation for particularly nomadic cultures. Many ancient shepherds actually slept in the fields with their sheep to protect them, likely more of a financial decision than a preference of locations to sleep.

The Bible is replete with Old Testament and New Testament examples about the shepherding of sheep. We know that a good shepherd would lead rather than drive the animals. A shepherd was attentive to the care of his sheep, his eyes always watchful for enemies of the sheep, such as predators or poachers. He remained vigilant for wild animals intent on feasting on the defenseless lambs.

There was also another, smaller yet just as serious, battle for the life of a sheep. Lice and ticks would find their way into the dense wool coats that covered sheep. Shepherds found that if unattended, these vermin could ultimately kill a sheep. They would make their way up from the woolly body to their head and ears. Once inside the ear, they could bring death to a valuable animal.

As always, throughout history, where there is a problem, innovative people have come up with a solution. Consequently, shepherds found that pouring oil on the head of the sheep and rubbing it in would make the skin and wool so slippery that infestation and death could be averted. This was called "anointing."

We are the Lord's sheep, and He is our shepherd.

When His Holy Spirit touches us, it is an anointing.

It is interesting to note that the enemy of our soul is not only our macro-challenge, or big problem, but many times he creates the micro-problems that can bring death. The Bible says that the "little foxes . . . spoil the vines" (Song 2:15). Small things can cause the collapse of a destiny. Impulsive decisions can become bad habits. Bad habits can become addictions. Addictions become idols that pull us away from God.

We are told in Scripture to not be ignorant of the Enemy's devices. While we're often concerned about wolves, or false teaching, the tiny lice will rise to strike us in unimaginable ways. Our ears become vulnerable to creative attacks and nuanced snares aimed at destroying our very lives. Our concerns for the big bad wolf can cause us to ignore the smaller threat of invasion upon our spiritual ears, causing us to lose our ability to hear our Shepherd. Jesus said that His sheep know His voice (John 10:27).

It's also noteworthy that the lice target the sheep's ears. Ears are the gateway to understanding and revelation. Jesus often said, "He who has ears to hear, let him hear!" (Matt. 11:15; 13:9). The Bible speaks to this gateway as an important entrance for faith to grow. Faith comes by hearing and hearing by the word of God. Just as sheep's anointing saved their lives, our spiritual anointing becomes a preventative and protective act to maintain keen hearing and a healthy life.

In fact, this is why our children should be introduced to the Holy Spirit and His power early in life. The precious ears of our children are subject to ideologies that may not line up with God's ways. The Holy Spirit's anointing upon young children will protect and shape them into cultural influencers that have access to the manifold wisdom of God. Pray over your children and maybe even periodically anoint them with oil. I pray often for my grandchildren for protection for what they hear and see. I simply say, "Lord, send Your anointing upon them!"

FILLED AND EMPOWERED

Over time, the act of anointing came to signify, in a broader sense, blessing, protection, and empowerment. It was highly adopted in its usage in biblical texts as the touch, or rub, of God. It also became a part of Jewish life and culture. Anointing, or pouring, of oil on the head has come to be used in official acts of inauguration, religious acts of commissioning, royal coronations, along with supernatural acts of healing and revelations, identifying God's presence on an individual.

The Holy Spirit became directly associated with the anointing in the New Testament. The Holy Spirit was indeed the oil. As we see in the book of Acts, Peter referred to the anointing with the Holy Spirit and power. He preached about "how God anointed Jesus of Nazareth with the Holy Spirit and with power, who went about doing good and healing all who were oppressed by the devil, for God was with Him" (Acts 10:38).

The anointing that Jesus had was the empowerment to do good and to subvert the powers of darkness. Although some scholars debate the beginning of Jesus' anointing, it seems to have been recognized by Jesus when He read from the scrolls in the synagogue. He had just returned from being baptized in the Jordan and was "filled with the Holy Spirit" and "led by the Spirit into the wilderness" (Luke 4:1). When Jesus returned forty days later, He came in the "power of the Spirit" (Luke 4:14). An incremental, continuous empowerment from the Spirit was definitely upon Christ throughout His time on earth.

WILD GOOSE CHASE

I fear that our view of the Holy Spirit and His power has thwarted our expectations of how dynamic the Christian life should be. The Holy Spirit is not the gentle dove that we all picture. He is gentle but also wild. The fifth-century Celts of Ireland called the Spirit of God the "Wild Goose." Michael Mitton, author of *Restoring the Woven Cord*, wrote, "Too many churches have wanted to domesticate the Holy Spirit, keeping this Wild Goose caged and safe by imposing rigid and controlling worship style in our Sunday worship . . . trapping our meetings with endless reports and feeding our people with tragically low expectations of what God can do in and through them."[1]

Acts, especially chapter 2, seems to confirm this wildness and rock the idea of a gentle Spirit. Whirlwinds, fire, and provoking tongues accompanied with great boldness began to set the disciples apart from their former selves. The authority and power that then accompanied the early church is such that it reportedly "turned the world upside down" (Acts 17:6).

There is also a great story in the Old Testament about the transfer of the Spirit. Moses was feeling the pressure from leading the multitudes of Israel to the land of promise. He literally told the Lord that the burden was too heavy. God responded with a plan. He told Moses to gather seventy elders and bring them to stand with him. He said, "I will take of the Spirit that is upon you and will put the same upon them" (Num. 11:17). This is a picture of consecration for those in positions of leadership. The obvious inference is that the anointing is transferable. When the Holy Spirit came upon them, they prophesied. Then as now, the anointing helps you do what you couldn't do before.

As it turned out, two of the men, Eldad and Medad, missed the meeting. Yet the Spirit of God hit them also. This example shows you the power of overflow. Proximity is important but not essential. God is eager that all experience this.

Unfortunately, then a problem emerged. Joshua complained that Eldad and Medad had not been at the required meeting (v. 26). Moses responded with this prophetic quote that rings through the ages, "Oh, that all the Lord's people were prophets and that the Lord would put His Spirit upon them!" (v. 29).

That was not the only example of an anointing in the Old Testament. The prophet Joel prophesied to a future of anointing: "It shall come to pass afterward that I will pour out My Spirit on all flesh; your sons and your daughters shall prophesy, your old men shall dream dreams, your young men shall see visions" (Joel 2:28).

Notice that the Spirit is poured out like oil. Peter later

acknowledged the fulfillment of this verse in Acts on the day of Pentecost, saying, "This is what was spoken by the prophet Joel" (Acts 2:16). It was a fulfillment of Moses' dream that total access to the Spirit's anointing would be offered to everyone.

From that day, the Holy Spirit has been impacting multitudes from generation to generation. The promise of the touch of the Holy Spirit and power is available to all who call upon the Lord. This touch will guide your life. This touch can exponentially raise your impact on this side of heaven. The touch of the Holy Spirit is a must in this present realm.

If you want more of God in your life, then cry out to the Lord for the secret sauce! Move your body to where it is. Get the oil of the Spirit, apply, and repeat if necessary. The anointing is a key. Your earthly actions in faith have heavenly consequences. God uses natural resources for supernatural purposes, if you're willing to be anointed by His Spirit!

YOUR VIEW FROM HERE

When the anointing of God is upon a person, it changes that individual from being a little ordinary person into being a giant.
—SUNDAY ADELAJA

1. Have you ever experienced an anointing of God's Spirit such as the one described at the Toronto church? Did you seek it out or did God seek you out? What did it feel like? How has it made a difference in your life? How does it continue to have an impact in your life?

2. How would you describe your relationship with the Holy Spirit presently in your faith journey? When have you witnessed evidence of the Spirit's power in your life? How did this manifest? When has God used you to demonstrate the power of His Spirit in the lives of others?

3. Set aside at least an hour and make a date with the Holy Spirit. If possible, take an entire afternoon or evening. After spending time in prayer asking the Spirit to guide you, unplug from everything else in your life and try to receive what the Spirit has for you. If you feel led to sing, then sing. If you feel compelled to read the Bible, trust the Spirit to guide you to the passage. If you feel overwhelmed with joy, then laugh. Spending dedicated time with God reinforces your desire to experience the full extent of his anointing power in your life.

> You love righteousness and hate wickedness;
> Therefore God, Your God, has anointed You
> With the oil of gladness more than Your
>   companions.
> —PSALM 45:7

CHAPTER 10

SPEAK THE LANGUAGE

Developing Rituals for Spiritual Blessing

Be quick to abstain from senseless traditions and
legends, but instead be engaged in the training of
truth that brings righteousness.
—1 TIMOTHY 4:7 TPT

Practice isn't the thing you do once you're good.
It's the thing you do that makes you good.
—MALCOLM GLADWELL

There is a certain minister, frequently on TV and radio, I love
to hear preach. When driving, I listen to him in my car most
of the time. He preaches a simple, yet powerful message that always
encourages. Listening to him as often as I do, I love the impact his

presentation of God's truth leaves on my heart. Frequently, I'll tell people to listen to him for thirty days and see what happens.

My adult son told me recently that he followed my recommendation and started listening to this minister when driving at work. My son loved what he heard and realized, as the days passed and became weeks, an inward change was taking place. He was being fed from the Word on a regular basis, and this diet was changing his life.

BEEN THERE, DONE THAT

Humans live in ritual. We get up and live our days in ritual. We eat at the same places, many times repeatedly, week after week. We work the same way, using habits established when we were much younger. We take the same routes home. We go to the same stores and buy the same products. We live according to the habits we practice. We do this for many reasons. Sometimes it is convenience, which can bring order and peace. Families build ritual through eating together, having movie nights, or vacationing at certain spots over and over again.

Rituals can take you to new waypoints. Rituals can create order in the midst of chaos. A peace comes with predictability. Doing the right things goes a long way. Many things are meant to be repeated over and over without losing their power. To build pathways, the early church created songs and creeds.

Rituals are not a replacement for divine encounters but rather a framework for them. Jesus can show Himself in spiritual ritual. Your obedience in pursuing the Lord systematically can shape you. In other words, a nonlegalistic, grace-filled ritual can bring forth an encounter because of the hunger of pursuit. An encounter can bring with it grace to begin or expand a spiritual ritual. Isn't it interesting that the word *spiritual* has *ritual* encased in it?

Your obedience and diligence can lead you to a place where you encounter God. When Jacob encountered God at Bethel, he said, "Surely the LORD is in this place, and I did not know it" (Gen. 28:16). In other words, God is in your future, waiting in certain places that will become waypoints in a new direction. Jacob thought he discovered something new, but he had nearly found a place of commitment that his grandfather Abraham had discovered years before. Similarly, Abraham's faithfulness prepared a place for his grandson to discover God. Can you imagine Jacob's shock when he found out that his grandfather built the old altar that was at Bethel?

You build a life of spiritual ritual and generations to come will benefit from it. Abraham started something that had a magnetic pull for generations. His obedience crafted a place for generations. Your waypoint may become an encounter spot for our children to come.

The movement toward a better life in Christ begins with encountering Him but is also perpetuated with the diligent hands of ordinary people. This key is often overlooked. In the Old Testament, when Joshua was in a battle, it was the combination of his sword and hailstones from heaven that won the day. The passage does note that more were killed from the hailstones than the sword. It's always more from heaven. You move and God moves. Your efforts of faith ignite a response from heaven.

MAKE IT MATTER

I fear that certain theologies have emerged in recent years that take all the energy out of believers moving intentionally. We have a generation of people waiting on God, while He may actually be waiting on us. Our empty personal rituals—surfing online, shopping, perpetual busyness—are shaping our hearts and taking us places we may not want to go ultimately. Gaming, Netflix, and social media can consume our focus and fill every moment with some kind of diversion or distraction.

These pursuits are not the producers of a successful or satisfying future. They may not be bad or evil, but they produce a ritualistic lifestyle, eventually programming your heart and mind in a different direction. They are not advancing anything in your life. In small measure they are entertaining. In great measure, they are all consuming. In order to establish sacred rituals that draw you closer to God, you must relinquish other habits that have been pulling you away. Tell your eyes not to look at that any longer. Tell your ears not to listen to harsh criticism, tell your feet to go where you tell them to go! The Bible says that missing the mark, or sin, will not be your master.

God loves the heart that responds in faith to pursue a godly life. I'm not talking about dead rituals or vain repetitions. I'm not even talking about the massive absorbing of the Bible. The Bible says that faith has substance and evidence. It is tangible. Build life-filled rituals that move you toward Christlikeness. In the past, the church has called these "spiritual disciplines."

If Jesus is not at the core of your intention, it will become dead. When you share the sacraments of communion, it can be dead. If you attach faith to it and do it ritualistically, you can become refreshed. Jesus said, "Do this in remembrance of me" (Luke 22:19 NIV). Years ago we changed our church's tradition of communion from once a month to every week. Those who take of it in faith, profit from it.

New Year's resolutions are famous for creating dead works. We start off at the beginning of the year with big plans. We attempt to read through the Bible in a year, but by day five we are exhausted and frustrated. How about taking one verse a week and committing it to memory, repeating it every day? I guarantee you your life will change over a year as you fill your soul with fifty-two life verses!

CLIMB THE LADDER

How do you establish spiritual ritual without becoming legalistically religious? How do you stay empowered by the Holy Spirit and not just your own personal discipline? You practice rituals while remembering that your encounters with God have given you all things that lead to an empowered and diligent life.

In Acts 1 we see this unwavering focus on God tested by tradition with the example of Peter. Even after Jesus ascended and Peter was waiting in the Upper Room, the temptation for tradition came. He was waiting in the room prescribed by Jesus. He interrupted the waiting with a church procedure to select a replacement for Judas. They cast lots to select the man of God as directed in the Old Testament. Matthias was recognized as the replacement, even though history has little to no record of his accomplishments afterward. Many believe that the apostle Paul was the spirit replacement for Judas. If true, Peter may have been relying on past ways to get things done rather than a new Spirit ritual.

Shortly after the Holy Spirit descended, however, new power brought new practices. New traditions and rituals began to emerge as the Holy Spirit began training the followers of Christ: "They continued steadfastly in the apostles' doctrine and fellowship, in the breaking of bread, and in prayers" (Acts 2:42).

Slowly, the waypoints of the past dropped off as they embraced a new Spirit-led reality. These became the new rituals. They began to learn a new way. Even their prejudice toward the Gentiles finally lost its grip (Acts 10). Peter recognized that there is no partiality between Jew and Gentile.

This is not an isolated example. Throughout Scripture, we are called to bring peace and reconciliation, to build something beautiful. Peter seemed to have an understanding that we indeed have the ability to build a great life, describing what has traditionally been called a "moral ladder" of progressive spiritual growth:

> For this very reason, giving all diligence, add to your faith virtue, to virtue knowledge, to knowledge self-control, to self-control perseverance, to perseverance godliness, to godliness brotherly kindness, and to brotherly kindness love. For if these things are yours and abound, you will be neither barren nor unfruitful in the knowledge of our Lord Jesus Christ. For he who lacks these things is shortsighted, even to blindness, and has forgotten that he was cleansed from his old sins. Therefore, brethren, be even more diligent to make your call and election sure, for if you do these things you will never stumble. (2 Peter 1:5–10)

The verses leading up to this ladder are all about the supernatural ability and power given to us in Christ. His divine power has given us all things that pertain to life and godliness. This is a revelation repeated throughout the New Testament. Apparently, the expectation and intention of God is for us to grow and move in progressive ways. In other words, God has given you everything you need to be a success in this life!

He also gave us promises that act as incentives to move us on this journey. The movement toward the promises creates an opportunity to become a partaker of His divine nature. This ladder allows us to climb toward our transformation into Christlikeness. We move from strength to strength, faith to faith, and glory to glory.

In the passage above, both verses 5 and 10 speak to diligence, anchoring the ladder from beginning to end. The Christian life has work attached to it. This work isn't for salvation, which can be achieved only through His precious blood. It is, though, a work of faith that moves you forward in your destiny.

SAME OLD ROUTINE

How do we move in His power to change our lives? We have all tried to be more moral, improve character, and break sin's effect. Jesus told us to learn of Him. Our life in Christ is one of creating rituals of Christlikeness to create lifestyles that reflect transformation.

There is definitely a difference between routine and ritual. Routine is essential for long-term peace and security on this side of heaven. Routine establishes our daily activities. We rise, eat, prepare, do, return, relax, and rest. It generally happens the same way, with slight variations every day. Routines are good. They create predictability, avoid cluttering the mind, and make a smooth path in front of us daily.

Ritual, on the other hand, is a supercharged routine and usually involves a ceremonial, weightier component. In Luke 11 when the disciples were asking to be trained in prayer, Jesus said, "When you pray, say . . ." (v. 2). This was not meant to become a vain repetition as some repeated phrases can become. After a time, the juice of the verse can be lost in religious repetition. Jesus was giving them an outline or a template to begin to honor God on a regular basis while making their request known.

The prayer that Jesus imparted is chock-full of layers of opportunity to beseech God. It has become known as "The Lord's Prayer." It begins with adoration, moves to commanding heaven's influence to earth, and continues into personal needs and protection. The capstone is similar to the opening, with a crescendo of adoration to the Lord. Rabbis at the time were known to offer prayer templates in order to further advance their followers. Jesus was apparently intending to give them a ritual that brings life and order in the midst of daily chaos.

Catholics have prioritized practices and rituals for millennia, preserving them from generation to generation, and they continue to offer to new generations a pathway of exploring God.

I'm convinced God responds to ritual because it involves intention. It cannot be an obedience that you believe will lead you to salvation. Only faith in the shed blood of Jesus will do that! For the disciples, though, repetition of Jesus' practices can deepen our knowledge and discernment in Christ.

In Acts 10 Cornelius was ritualistically mimicking the Jews in faith, and it attracted the attention of heaven. I could argue that his desire to find God by copying the Jewish lifestyle of giving alms and praying to God opened a grand door for him and all Gentiles. Hunger is always a key in everything you do. If you hunger after God, you will be filled.

Routine, if done in faith, becomes a ritual that can produce fruit. It is a form of preparing and positioning yourself before God. The epistles inform and coach us over and over again about how to live our lives. Ritual is a way to order our progress.

STICKING POWER

Sticking power has become a big issue in business. Many books have been written to help make products or services stick in the minds of potential consumers. The kingdom of God in some ways is similar. When I taught a course to improve people's speaking skills or human relations, I used a simple formula to help them create stickiness. I taught them to give information, then demonstration, and ultimately activation. This progression has different stickiness at each level.

INFORMATION

Information is needed and yet can drift from your mind easily. Facts and data can become mental Post-it notes that stick enough to hold an item in place yet is easily removed.

DEMONSTRATION

Demonstration is slightly stickier. When you see something demonstrated, it holds more firmly in your memory. Many of us can recount stories of things we have witnessed that impacted us or wowed us. When you demonstrate what you are trying to teach, it creates stickier glue, maybe more like household glue. You remember it well, but it may not alter your activities or lifestyle. Although demonstration is stickier, it can still be removed from your memory.

Jesus was amazing at giving out information and demonstrating to His disciples exactly what lifestyle and actions He was expecting. Actually, He commented that they would do even greater things.

ACTIVATION

The strongest glue of all, though, is activation. You can hear and watch all day long, learning everything you might need to know about something, but there is nothing like actually doing it. I can learn about places all around the world through pictures, but my strongest mental images are those of me standing in front of the Tower of Pisa or Big Ben. I can sit and talk about many things I've learned by direct experience, with traveling being one of my favorite ways to practice activation. Those experiences become the glue! Consistent repetition with full engagement bonds you to the activity. It's the duct tape and superglue of spiritual growth. Practice may not make perfect, but practicing the presence of God leads you to the perfect One every time.

When you decide to get out of the grandstands and step onto the field, I can predict your future. You may get battered, but you will grin widely through the mud even if you're missing a tooth! Transformation comes when you do something, especially if it leads you to Christ.

Jesus' parable brings clarity to the meaning of stickiness with the parable of the houses built on sand and rock (Matt. 7:24–27). What does it practically look like to build on sand? Those who "hear only" are building sand castles. There is a sense of structure, but it is merely sand that the wind can easily blow away. It feels good and brings accomplishment but is only temporary and nothing eternal will stand.

Alternatively, those who hear and then do are the builders who last. The *do* is the glue that holds our destiny together. The rains and the floods of life may come, and the winds will blow, but the house on the rock stands firm. This is the wisdom of God! You are wise to create a life of ritual, a lifetime of pattern building in which you hear what Jesus has said and structure your life around it.

SPIRIT-ENERGIZED PREPARATION

Rituals also help us prepare for the future God has for us. We are His temple, His holy people to demonstrate the love and mercy of God, and our lives have to align with that call. What does it mean to make your path straight, fill the valleys, and so forth? Again, it is a divine partnership of God's power in an earthen vessel. You are called for constant improvement by His power.

Spiritual rituals do not get you to heaven, but they become your gift to an amazing Savior. Your worship rituals are thanks in faith to a great God. The Bible says that as we behold Him, we are being transformed into the same image (2 Cor. 3). When you make a ritual of worship, it invites transformation.

Soaking in the Bible also brings change. Gathering with other Christians brings change. Prayer brings change. Giving regularly softens your heart and heals your finances. Touching the poor by extending your soul creates light in your own life. Doing what Jesus called you to do creates pathways to greater joy, peace, and clarity.

Jesus entreats us: "Learn from me, for I am gentle and humble in heart, and you will find rest for your souls" (Matt. 11:29 NIV).

The life in Jesus is meant to be simple and powerful. Religion, on the other hand, makes things complicated. Jesus is light and easy. Jews had an oral tradition that there were 613 commandments in the Torah, the five books of Moses of the Pentateuch. After Jesus' death and the destruction of Jerusalem, Jews became concerned about the carrying on of oral tradition. The seeds of the Talmud (a word literally meaning "learning") were sown, as writings began to record all that entailed the customs emerging around the Torah. The Talmud includes the 613 commandments believed to be in the Torah. In standard print the Talmud is more than six thousand pages long!

Throughout history, religion tends to grow more complex. Jesus upended expectations and sent the Holy Spirit as a breath of fresh air. The Jews had created complicated systems, but Jesus took the Ten Commandments and condensed them into only two: love God and love your neighbor. This perfectly sums up a life in Christ. I'm not proposing the *do* as a new law but as a Spirit-energized preparation before God.

THE LOVE LINE

The following chart shows the love line that originated with Jesus. Through His shed blood, His love has dripped down on us creating a way to heaven. The chart illustrates that it is easy to get off course into the law or lawlessness. Sin attracts us to the left and dead religion to the right. Decisions will cause you to veer from the centrality of God's love. Either way, it ends badly. Sin will create a lifestyle that can destroy you. Religion can produce pride and take you from the love of Jesus. You must continue with your eyes fixed on Jesus. You will have waypoints to rest and refresh. If you get off track, you can repent and turn back to His love. You can also build spiritual rituals to turn you back to Jesus. He's always there, waiting.

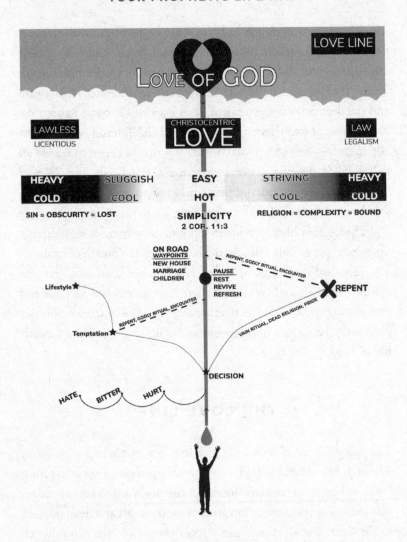

The line down the middle of this chart represents the love of God expressed in the sending of Jesus Christ. It touches us and begins a path to heaven we call the "Love Line." Veering to the left we find sin, or separation from God. Sin, initiated by yielding to temptation, is always a decision or choice. It can also occur during a hurt that grows into bitterness and ultimately hate. These decisions move you further from God's great love. Life gets complicated outside of the love of God, but the simplicity of Jesus helps keep you on track.

The right side of the chart speaks to the error of replacing the spiritual with religion. Religion is an expression of belief and with it a temptation to move toward knowledge of tradition rather than Jesus. There is nothing wrong with tradition as long as it doesn't rob you of relationship with Him. In fact, most churches originally tried to build traditions and ritual to focus on Jesus, but some of it got lost over the centuries.

The chart shows the coldness of religion without relationship. Vain religion will rob you. When you find yourself in this place, then immediately repent, and begin to move back to the centrality of Jesus and His love. The right church is important for growth; the wrong church could cool your passion for Jesus. Fix your eyes on Jesus and enjoy the fullness of Christ!

PATTERNS OF PURPOSE

Through the practice of sacred rituals, we can grow closer to Jesus as we follow His teachings. Consistently using spiritual practices enables you to maintain your focus on the life God calls you to live. They become facilitators and conduits for the power of the Holy Spirit. Through them you're reminded to take up your cross and follow Christ, renewing your mind rather than allowing it to be conformed to the world.

A healthy approach to Christ-centered habits can open new revelations and create a more blessed life. Your simple obedience in creating rituals of growth will push you forward toward your destiny. We see this illustrated when God spoke to Joshua as he was preparing to enter the promised land, the place fulfilling God's promises for His people:

Only be strong and very courageous, that you may *observe to do* according to all the law which Moses My servant commanded you; do not turn from it to the right hand or to the left, that you may prosper wherever you go. This Book of the Law shall not depart from your mouth, but you shall meditate in it day and night, that you *may observe to do* according to all that is written in it. For then you will *make your way prosperous*, and then you will have good success. (Josh. 1:7–8, my emphasis)

The attentive and intentional Christian who is encountering God and moving on a Jesus-centered track will prosper. Joshua used the *do* that is the glue to become prosperous and obtain a successful life. He created a life of listening, watching, and doing. Note the key words in the text: *meditate*, *observe*, and *do*. Your life of discipline and repetition create ritual that brings life and success. Look for ways to create patterns and systems for growth and then prepare to experience the fullness of your prophetic life through the power of God's Spirit.

YOUR VIEW FROM HERE

Devotion is a certain act of the will by which man gives himself promptly to divine service.
—SAINT THOMAS AQUINAS

1. Describe any sacred rituals you currently practice that are helping you grow in your faith. How did you begin to use these rituals? How often do you practice them? What is it about doing these rituals that draws you closer to God and the presence of His Spirit?

2. How would you distinguish between routines and rituals? In your current journey of faith, do you rely more on one than the other? How can you prevent rituals from losing their power and fading into routines? What does "do is the glue" mean for you?

3. As we see in this chapter, rituals, when used in faith, can facilitate encounters and spiritual blessings. Think again about how you currently use spiritual practices to nurture and nourish your relationship with God. What is at least one daily ritual you can develop to create a new pathway to God's presence? Ask the Holy Spirit to guide you as you consider adding a new, regular practice to your spiritual life.

Practice these things, immerse yourself in them, so that all may see your progress.
—1 Timothy 4:15 esv

CHAPTER 11

TOUR GUIDE

Following Where the Spirit Leads

The Lord will *guide you* continually,
and satisfy your soul in drought,
and strengthen your bones;
you shall be like a watered garden,
and like a spring of water, whose waters do not fail.
—ISAIAH 58:11

One of the greatest values of mentors is the ability
to see ahead what others cannot see and to help
them navigate a course to their destination.
—JOHN C. MAXWELL

God is your ultimate Guide on your journey of faith. Through His Holy Spirit, He provides counsel and enlightenment for your many decisions throughout life. In fact, the Bible is full of references to the guiding power of the Spirit of God. In the familiar Psalm 23, we see phrases like "He leads me" and "He makes me," illustrating the active influence of protective guidance for any follower of Jesus.

Jesus Himself overtly referred to the Holy Spirit as our Guide when He said, "However, when He, the Spirit of truth, has come, He will guide you into all truth; for He will not speak on His own authority, but whatever He hears He will speak; and He will tell you things to come" (John 16:13). Throughout Scripture, the Holy Spirit emerges as a revealer of hidden truth, as the apostle Paul said, "God has revealed them [unseen things] to us through His Spirit. For the Spirit searches all things, yes, the deep things of God" (1 Cor. 2:10).

BEACONS OF WISDOM

When we think about being led by God's Spirit, we're usually wrestling with life's big decisions. We want to know where to go to college, what job to take, whether to date someone, how to grow closer to our spouse, or when to move to another home. One of the best models for decision-making that I've ever run across comes from Bob Mumford's book *Take Another Look at Guidance.*[1] In it he compares making life choices with a certain harbor in Italy that has three guiding lights. All three lights must align or disaster is certain for any boat entering the harbor. Based on this metaphor, Mumford's three beacons of wisdom for sailing into godly solutions for life's major decisions are:

- The Word of God (Objective)
- The Holy Spirit (Subjective)
- The Circumstances (Confirmative)

This simple yet profound method works amazingly well, and I've referred to it for more than forty years. Based on Mumford's model, I have often taken this mental quiz when facing a crossroads:

- Although it may not be specifically mentioned in the Bible, does it agree with the general principles of God's Word? Does it conflict with biblical understanding?
- Does this feel right in my spirit? Or do I feel that warning in my heart that I feel when I make wrong choices? Is peace present in my process?
- Finally, are the circumstances aligning with what I have been sensing? God will make a way. If alignment doesn't occur, it may not be the correct choice or the right timing.

Whether or not you find these three beacons and questions helpful, you will discover that God communicates His leadership in a variety of ways. Building a relationship with the Holy Spirit will open your life to direct access of wisdom in numerous ways. The Bible will become a guide for your path and create wisdom and empowerment for the bigger choices in life.

God will also bring trusted friends and advisors for you to confer with. The Bible tells us, "Without counsel, plans go awry, but in the multitude of counselors they are established" (Prov. 15:22). Some of your counselors, such as pastors, parents, or teachers, have already had influence in your life. Their wisdom often lingers through time. Their words and deeds become an example that resonates powerfully throughout your entire life. But there are also times in your life when the wisdom of the Spirit compels you to seek assistance from other people.

GUIDANCE COUNSELORS

Looking back, I have developed numerous guides in my life. Some of them were birthed out of organic relationships and others emerged in more deliberate, professional settings. Whether you visit them in their office or treat them to a casual lunch, many professionals love to help give you insight based on their expertise. Business owners, bankers, accountants, artists, and entrepreneurs are often willing to become mentors or friends, providing a relational context for their shared information. The best guides for your life will care about you and want to look out for you and your best interests. These are the ones who will pray, guide, instruct when asked, and support you even in troubled times.

The best guides often reflect the wisdom and grace of God. They display an innate desire to create solutions and help others discover how to move forward. If their motives are wrong, their help can easily become manipulation. But true guides will empty themselves and invest all they are in the success of another. They have passed where you are and know the pitfalls and challenges. While they're not perfect, they've learned a thing or two and want to help others know what they wished someone had told them.

A spiritual guide is able to understand the timing of when you need advice and when you need silence, and that a listening ear is essential. A godly guide will lead you to truth, either pointing you specifically to God's Word or presenting fundamental principles from the Bible. This kind of guide will speak with authority yet not be an authoritarian. These guides will impart truth that is beyond them. The goal of a Spirit-led guide is to help you find your own way, trusting that God is already at work in your life.

PUT ME IN, COACH!

Today it's quite popular to get a life coach. Many even specialize, so you can enlist business coaches, marriage coaches, financial coaches, and fitness coaches. While I'm personally excited about the explosive market for coaches, I'm also cautious when it comes to actually choosing a coach. Ideally, you want a person you trust, typically a professional or expert with some kind of credentials and experience. They've gone through some training or certification. In many cases, their success is self-evident. I recommend going to guides who are successful at what you want to do. If it's finances or investing, follow the wealthy. If it's marriage, follow the happy couple who has been married for more than twenty or thirty years.

Finding a community of other believers is also essential for growth and guidance. I belong to a prophetic church, Bethel Cleveland, a community of spiritual explorers. They actually believe that God interacts with His people. They lean into it and do not shrink back. These people are significant in one another's lives because of their depth of experience in the Spirit. With my church family, I can share wild ideas and even greenhouse them within our congregation. Sometimes they fail and sometimes they thrive, but what an incubator of creativity it is! People are conquering their cultural mountains right before our eyes. If you want to find Spirit-loving people to do life with, then find a Spirit-loving church.

God will also use people in your life who may not be believers. When I had a bone marrow transplant in 2013, I chose the best specialists. My doctors may have been Christians, but I didn't check. It would be great, but it was not a part of my criteria. Under the circumstances, I wanted the best medical professionals in their field. God uses all kinds of people to guide us. Don't be afraid to seek out individuals who can provide insight and expertise even if they may not share your faith.

Learn from those willing to pour into you. A reasonable process is always geared toward the maturity and liberation of the student. I have raised up prophetic teams all over the world. Wherever I have gone, I have preferred to take teams with me. This provides continued experience for them while blessing a group of recipients.

When I was a business instructor, we taught that good coaching involved being directive. There is a season where you are more overt in creating course corrections. When my teams are functioning, I watch them. I'm direct with them because I'm creating a system that will serve them for years to come.

When they are maturing, I switch to consulting or coaching. I've built a level of trust, and we now can consult regarding ways and means of ministering to a particular scenario. Consulting involves oversight, while allowing a greater freedom. The ultimate goal is a commissioning or release, which we call "free reign." Under free reign, a person can begin to take teams on their own as ambassadors of our church or ministry. Some move quickly through this process, and others enjoy remaining part of a larger team.

SEVEN IS ENOUGH

The following seven sectors of life will demand additional insights from the Lord through the Holy Spirit and through godly connections and relationships. These are the areas most prone to myriad decisions that affect your everyday life. They inherently challenge you because of the possible directions you may choose to go. Consequently, they're often filled with challenges, obstacles, and unexpected land mines that require help from others in order to navigate.

GEOGRAPHY

Many people believe choosing the location where you live to be the most important decision of life outside of a spiritual rebirth. Think about it. Everything is determined or influenced by geography: where you work, who you marry, your income, your health and attitude, and much more. Obviously in today's virtual, off-site jobs, some can live anywhere and do whatever. But geography still has a big influence.

Ancient Christians believed that "place" was sacred. You may have experienced places that felt sacred to you as well as others that caused you distress. Trust that God has a place for you. Where is the place that feeds your soul and provides the best opportunities for advancement, peace, and community? While geography is important, your location should become a means, not an end. In other words, de-spiritualize your geography because trusting God can and will move anywhere. We believe in revival, but the truth is, you are revival! God's presence goes with you wherever you go. Take what you have, and search for a place in God.

God will direct you, stop you, and more than likely, favor you. Please do not get stuck somewhere and create a theology that says God wants you to suffer geographically. You have been set free, so act like a liberated person. While God does direct certain people to stay put where they are, this is often for a specific season. Seek the Spirit and not just a city, suburb, or split-level. Find a place that fits you. Dream, roam, settle, and love your locale!

SPOUSES

I have given similar advice regarding life mates for forty years: when dating, do not propose marriage for at least four seasons, preferably more. My present wife, Cindy, needed to see me in spring, summer, fall, and winter. People shift seasonally, and I needed to see her in each of a year's four seasons as well.

Even with compatibility during the various seasons, many challenges exist in a godly relationship. It's a long list due to the great importance of marriage. They would include things like your fiancé's background, environment, temperament, education, personality, life experiences, and on and on. Long periods of dating may be necessary, with a shorter engagement to plan the wedding.

MONEY

Studies show over and over again that money can be a fringe benefit of happiness but rarely if ever its source. In the book *Who's*

Your City? the author cites studies demonstrating, "It's not that people with money are happier; it's that happier people may be better earners."[2] In fact, studies from the National Academy of Sciences in 2010 revealed that a household income above $75,000 per year "does nothing for happiness, enjoyment, sadness or stress."[3]

Money is important and often tests our faithfulness. How we view our finances usually reflects something about how we view God and our roles in His kingdom. Jesus told His followers:

> Whoever can be trusted with very little can also be trusted with much, and whoever is dishonest with very little will also be dishonest with much. So if you have not been trustworthy in handling worldly wealth, who will trust you with true riches? And if you have not been trustworthy with someone else's property, who will give you property of your own? (Luke 16:10–12 NIV)

There is a direct correlation in Scripture between faithfulness in money and the eternal, spiritual realm. What you do with money matters for eternity. Those things that are associated with money are therefore an important test of faithfulness. Your job is nothing but an exchange. You give your blood, sweat, and tears in exchange for currency. Your labor is your currency. Your gifts, talent, mind, and strength are currencies of your faithfulness. If you are faithful to labor, you should receive compensation.

Biblically, if you are faithful with your currency on earth, God promotes that openness to true riches—spiritual riches! What an excellent motivation to handle money well! Your honesty, charity, and generosity open doors to earth and heaven. The true riches are in heaven and available on the other side of faithfulness. Your "test of money" can become a "testimony!"

Learn to honor what God has given you. Regarding money, treat it with respect because it is a school for heavenly riches, and the Father watches what we do with it.

Learn to earn well. Learn to save and invest. Read books on financial wisdom, study God's Word, and handle well the bounty you've been given, knowing your faithfulness will be compensated from heaven's bank.

Mentors can play pivotal roles in how we learn to handle money. Seek out expert advice on investments, retirement, insurance, and estate planning.

FRIENDS

The Bible says that true friends are few. You'll recall from our previous chapter how those Irish Celt early Christians associated with Saint Patrick called life's few special friends *anam cara*. The *anam cara* soul friend understood and accepted you and "was a person to whom you could reveal the hidden intimacies of your life."[4]

In the Celtic church, this soul friend was generally a teacher, companion, or spiritual guide. It generally referred to someone who was your confessor, someone you trusted with every aspect of your life. Your friendship was an entrustment, an agreement of privacy, honor, and respect for the soul of a person.

For us today, soul friends still create a security and a sense of belonging. With my various soul friends, I get with some often and others periodically. They hold something for me and I for them. They know me and love me for who I am becoming. They are a bulwark in times of crisis and challenge. Celts believed that when you were understood, you were home. Look at the quality of your friendships and seek out your *anam cara*!

EDUCATION

I used to say that everyone needed a degree. The crippling debt that has come out of pursuing a promising education, however, is alarming.

Generally speaking, though, education is always beneficial. It doesn't have to be formal but can simply reflect a lifelong curiosity in all facets of God's creation. Sometimes your education may be specific to the task pursued, while others are general prep for a myriad of opportunities. Develop an attitude that seeks to learn from everyone around you.

Jesus would have had extensive training in the local synagogue as well as on-the-job training with His earthly father, Joseph. Jesus probably started His occupational training as early as twelve or thirteen. He was widely networked in the Jewish community, and much of His educational destiny was set.

But God often uses people for different fields than ones for which they're trained. Peter was an uneducated fisherman. That does not mean he wasn't intelligent. He was a business owner. Skilled at fishing, he knew his boat was his business. Jesus selected him to lead the emerging Jewish church in Jerusalem. The religiously untrained, uneducated one, Peter, was selected to lead the legalistic and intelligent Jews in the religious hot spot of Jerusalem.

Paul, on the other hand, was an expert in Judaism. Yet Paul was commissioned to the non-Jews, the Gentiles mostly outside of Israel, in the expanding church. His brilliance positioned him to be a debater with other brilliant thinkers, yet the Jewish component of his life was secondary to his mission.

In your journey of faith, your preparation in one area may transition you into a totally different field for an entirely different audience as you follow the voice of the Lord. So become a lifelong learner, and God will weave your wisdom into a beautiful tapestry of opportunity. Your responsibility is to prepare, because God will always use what you have and provide what you need.

CAREER

Most of the time, your education, experience, certification, and licensure lead you into a career. Some jobs will be planned and others will emerge. Regardless, you should work as unto the Lord and give your best. We're told, "Whatever your hand finds to do, do it with all your might" (Eccl. 9:10 NIV).

Work is important in order to care for yourself and family, build your confidence, and affect the world around you. Never allow yourself to stay in an unoccupied role for long. Ed Silvoso, author of *Anointed for Business*, wrote, "Make peace with your job by accepting it as God's starting point for you."[5] Institutional systems are never perfect, and many may seem grossly imperfect, but accept where God has positioned you. We're called to join the system with the same attitude as Daniel and Joseph in the Bible. Despite the unfairness and injustice in their respective situations, they remained faithful and trusted God. As a result, God used them in mighty ways! He will do the same with you.

Bring the kingdom of heaven to the kingdom of your career. Most of the Old Testament characters were in oppressive circumstances that limited their boundaries and power. They found and thrived supernaturally to shape kingdoms and change leadership's mind. You are the missionary to a career. The eighteenth-century missionary William Carey said, "My business is to preach the gospel; I repair shoes to pay expenses."

Pick something, move forward, and watch God shape you!

WELLNESS

While wellness is a broad category encompassing our physical, mental, emotional, and spiritual well-being, it also requires making Spirit-led decisions. Scripture tells us to use our senses to discern things of God rather than worldly matters: "Solid food is for the mature, who by constant use have trained themselves to distinguish good from evil" (Heb. 5:14 NIV).

Usually, we must train our senses in this kind of spiritual discernment. You learn to trust the Spirit's guidance regarding what is best for you and what will harm you. Your reborn spirit is in charge of subjecting your senses to God's Word and obeying His ways. As mature Christians we learn to win in our own lives by surrendering all aspects of our beings to the Lord. What you see, hear, sense, touch, and taste can guide you only if it's brought into alignment with God.

Your wellness speaks of spirit, soul, and body. Nourishing, developing, and exercising each area require intentional habits. You must not neglect one dimension at the expense of another. Pay attention to your body and what it needs to be healthy—nutritious food, lots of water, regular exercise, fresh air, and adequate sleep. Provide your mind with intellectual stimulation as you utilize the gift of intelligence God has given you.

Finally, pay attention to your spiritual growth and its relationship to all the other parts of you. Make choices today that train your spirit by reading the Word and relying on prayer. Build your soul with various seasons of rest, improvement, and meditation. Your wellness ultimately resides in your relationship with God. When you put Him first and follow His Spirit, then you will remain attentive to all the different aspects of your being. You are created in God's image, so live like it.

LISTEN CAREFULLY

You are building your life based on choices. In the loud clamor of so many voices vying for your attention, it can be hard to know whom to trust, whom to listen to, and whom to follow. Those around you continue shouting what needs to be done, according to them. So many voices cry out to be your guide, often pulling you in opposing directions. But the Spirit's voice is the only one that gives you life. Learn to listen carefully to hear His gentle whisper and the silent utterances that speak straight into your heart.

The kingdom of God is built on righteousness, peace, and joy. Your senses are designed to help you worship and serve your Creator. When you use them to pursue God, then they show you different insights into His character. Experiencing these revelations requires those sacred rituals we discussed in our previous chapter. Basically, we must exercise them in ways that produce spiritual muscle. Training in godliness will exercise your senses to resist counsel that will steer you wrong.

Choose your advisors wisely. Learn to navigate the challenges of life by building community with other pilgrims as you learn to listen to the Holy Spirit. He will lead you through life's many twists and turns, pointing the way and keeping you moving in God's direction. Like a divine Tour Guide from God's kingdom, the Spirit wants to share His wisdom, passion, and joy with you.

YOUR VIEW FROM HERE

The greatest good you can do for another is not just to share your riches but to reveal to him his own.
—Benjamin Disraeli

1. How often do you seek the Holy Spirit's guidance when making important decisions in your life? How does He usually communicate with you regarding such guidance? When was the last time you sensed His leading as you faced a significant crossroad?

2. Who are the people God has most frequently used to encourage, guide, and speak into your life? What are some of the big life lessons you've learned from them? How do they continue to give you direction and

support? Who are the people presently in your life who provide coaching, mentoring, and training for you? How can you pass along what you've learned to others?

3. After spending a few minutes in prayer, inviting the Spirit to guide you, list the seven big life areas covered in this chapter. Grab your journal or a notebook and reflect on each category. How has God given you direction regarding that topic or issue? How would you describe where you are presently in regard to each area? How would you like to grow in each of these specific arenas? Review your Boom Loop that you drafted at the end of chapter 8. How can it help you make decisions within each of these categories? After you've reviewed all seven and set at least one goal for each, arrange a meeting with a trusted soul friend, your *anam cara*, to go over your plan.

A man of many companions may come to ruin, but there is a friend who sticks closer than a brother.
—PROVERBS 18:24 ESV

CHAPTER 12

A COMPLETE ROUND

Planting Seeds and Bearing Fruit

> Every good gift and every perfect gift is from
> above, and comes down from the Father of
> lights, with whom there is no variation or shadow
> of turning.
> —JAMES 1:17

> God never loses sight of the treasure which He
> has placed in our earthen vessels.
> —CHARLES SPURGEON

Golf has to be one of the most nuanced games in history. I love to golf—well, except when I don't. I'm not a hacker, but I'm also not awesome. A few years ago, I took it up on a more serious level, initially, because a local golf course offered specials to ministers, and I thought it would be a good date with my wife each week. Playing regularly was bittersweet. Some days I felt I could have been a serious golfer if I had taken it up earlier in my life, and other days I had to restrain myself from swearing.

My father-in-law was an avid golfer, strong and consistent in his game despite poor eyesight. His sight was so bad that others had to watch where his ball landed. Nonetheless, he was generally the best player in any foursome. Whenever I golfed with him, he took the game seriously and expected others to do the same. He knew the rules and was the "golf sheriff." Among his many sayings surrounding the culture of golf, he frequently exclaimed, "Playing nine holes is not golf!"

Like I said, he was passionate about the game.

HOLY IN ONE

My father-in-law knew that if you're a serious golfer, nine holes is not an indicator of your true game. Playing more frequently these past few years, I have a better understanding of what he meant. He held firmly to the belief that if you really want to play the game as it was intended to be played, then you committed to the full eighteen. After all, we can call miniature golf or Topgolf "golf," but most would agree that it's not the same thing as a real round of golf on an actual course. Similarly, we can play disc or Frisbee golf, but no one would claim it's the same game played at Augusta or Pebble Beach or St. Andrews. These derivative versions may be fun, but true golf is on a course with rules and eighteen holes of play.

There is a reason for this designation. We could think that most of our strength and skill might be used up in the first nine holes, which would mean that the second nine should be very different from the first nine. And as a frequent average golfer, I would concur that on many courses, the second nine is more challenging. Many times, however, I actually play better on the second nine due to becoming loosened up and more in the rhythm of my game. Plus, we must remember that the highest level of regular-play golf consists of eighteen holes. Regardless of the much-debated topic of each individual's golf game, eighteen remains the standard measure of a person's talent.

Golf must be important to me because it was actually a crucial part of the dream I described in chapter 6, the one that left me in extended laughter for several hours. What I didn't mention was the prominence of a golf ball, which was the central object in the dream. When I awoke, I was puzzled and unclear as to its meaning.

Later on that day, however, a known prophetic man named Robin McMillan called me. We share such encounters with each other often, mainly because we believe they're from God. How fun it is to have a community of likeminded, crazy believers! Robin is a treasure on multiple levels, and when I shared my laughing dream with him that morning, I mentioned the golf ball. He immediately said, "Ah, that's the nines."

"What do you mean?" I said.

"The nines. You know, the front nine and the back nine," he explained. "They are the gifts of the Spirit and the fruit of the Spirit—two nines equal eighteen!"

As he was telling me this, I repeated it out loud over the phone. My wife, Cindy, overheard me and said, "Wait, what's the date today?" I checked and it was February 9, 2018—or 2/9/18! This was no coincidence, but what I've come to recognize as a punctuation mark from God. He was confirming my friend Robin's interpretation. Even without fully understanding, I knew that God was up to something, revealing and clarifying His message to me one piece at a time.

ON THE LINKS

My golf parable continued to unfold, even after my dream and Robin's interpretation. Several months later a young minister from Florida, who happened to be a former professional golfer, was speaking at our church. In casual conversation, he inquired as to any of my recent revelations. Naturally, knowing his expertise, I went with the golf ball dream. Without hesitation, he said, "Ah, the front nine and the back nine." He continued, "The front nine and the back nine are the gifts and the fruit. And, yes, 2018 is the year of the Spirit!"

I remember wondering if everyone knew this but me. He then went on to show me a text from a nationally known minister who had shared the exact same terminology just the week before. I was shocked! It never ceases to amaze me how detailed God can be when getting an important message across.

A month later, I was ministering at a church in eastern Ohio. I was training them in the prophetic and was using a collage of photos already on their projected screen. They had downloaded it off the internet, and I had never seen it before. In one of the exercises, we partnered up and selected one of the pictures on the screen to act as a prompt to talk to one another. Because God often uses pictures, it was meant to familiarize people with how to describe what God shows us. I use this and many similar activities like training wheels on a bicycle to help aspiring believers grow in their awareness of God's presence and the movement of the Holy Spirit.

Their worship leader, my partner for this exercise, came over to me and selected a picture of two interlocking chain links. As he was saying what he thought God was showing him, I became fixated on the picture of the links. They were two open-ended chain links yet still connected. Then it hit me—the links looked like two nines! I also remembered that golf courses are called "links," like in a chain. It was another reminder of what God was trying to tell me.

Since then, I'm still getting more revelations regarding my golf dream. Basically, I believe that the Spirit of God gives us gifts (the front nine) for us to move in. We find these listed in 1 Corinthians 12:7–11. The Spirit's intention, of course, is to reveal and cultivate a greater awareness of Jesus in us. The second nine, the fruit of the Spirit—found in Galatians 5:22–23—emerge from using our gifts.

I'm convinced the nine gifts of the Spirit are powerful tools to impact those around us while also providing a cutting edge for our personal maturation. It's important to be a Holy Spirit–led person in order to move into deeper maturity. Traditionally in the American version of Christianity, the gifts of the Spirit are seen as the "shallow end of the pool," as it were. We have all witnessed people with great spiritual giftings yet shallow foundations. We hold the fruit of the Spirit in more esteem because we equate them with maturity. But what if the two are related?

FREE GIFTS

The Bible speaks of spiritual gifts in a number of places, but particularly in 1 Corinthians 12. There, Paul instructs us not to be ignorant. In other words, these gifts are a big part of the arsenal that God has given you in your spiritual walk. These nine gifts are diverse but of the same Spirit. A gift is given, not earned. Consequently, they are given to the mature and immature. While one or two gifts may be keener in some individuals, the truth is, we all have access to the Spirit. In other words, you might move in all these gifts at one time or another, or see multiple gifts occurring at once. And it's highly likely that you will focus on the gifts you feel more comfortable with and focus heavier on developing them.

The follow-up paragraphs (vv. 12–31) show diversity in the members of the body as well as their giftings. Various people from vastly different backgrounds make up the church, and they are all important. Basically, the apostle Paul demonstrated the multiple expressions within the body of Christ. It's as if he was saying, "Don't try to categorize or rely on stereotypes!" Spirit-filled people will be used in many ways—as the Spirit deems necessary.

Frequently, I see these gifts distributed just as needed, used by imperfect people who have access to a warehouse of opportunity for exercising their particular gifts. There are no qualifications for being used by God this way other than being born of the Spirit. The gifts are indiscriminate. Gifts from God come whether you are rich or poor, old or young, freely offered to every color, creed, or gender.

The gifts are seen as the manifestation of the Spirit in the believer. Consequently, gifts are to be expected in the life of a Christian. We can tell the Spirit is on a person who exhibits these kinds of gifts. Your maturation level is apparently irrelevant. People who demonstrate gifts of the Spirit originate in the Spirit, even if they are immature in other ways. We're told that "the manifestation of the Spirit is given to each one for the profit of all" (1 Cor. 12:7).

The Spirit of God brings these gifts in order to profit everyone! The Bible likes the word *edify*, which means "to build up or strengthen." This manifestation of the Spirit is to build up—both in us and in others. The seeds of the Spirit sown in other individuals will bear fruit. They will be built up and transformed! God is glorified as our gifts point back to Him and His power.

ON THE BACK NINE

In light of my dream and what God has revealed to me, the release of spiritual gifts can move a person into the "back nine." When you're being faithful in healing, word of wisdom, or other gifts, then it can open a pathway for maturity in another. Using your gifts produces fruit in yourself as well as in others. Sharing your gifts will plant seeds in the soil of another's heart. If the ground is plowed and ready in that person, then a seed can be planted and eventually bear fruit—the fruit of the Spirit.

Such spiritual pollination demonstrates our dependence on one another. It is important to sow seeds indiscriminately and know that some will yield an incredible harvest of spiritual fruit! Using your gifts to plant seeds in others also demonstrates the grace of God. He is willing to take risks on imperfect people in order to shape them toward godliness.

For example, just yesterday I heard that a friend of mine was discouraged. He and his wife have followed a word from the Lord to move to another state. Quickly they ran into various challenges. But I reminded him that sometimes difficulty is attached to the release of a gift, as we see in this summary from Scripture:

> He sent a man before them—
> Joseph—who was sold as a slave.
> They hurt his feet with fetters,
> He was laid in irons.
> Until the time that his word came to pass,
> The word of the LORD tested him.
>
> (Ps. 105:17–19)

The release of God's intention can create challenge in your life. Joseph had been given an epic dream about his destiny. That dream and the confession of it brought a boatload of difficulty. This passage speaks to the involvement of God in creating an atmosphere of growth and maturation. As painful as it was, that atmosphere shaped Joseph into who he needed to be in order to fulfill what was spoken in the dream.

CLOSING THE GAP

Be careful what you dream. There is a "shaping gap" between the dream and the fulfillment. Closing this gap becomes the transition to the back nine. No matter what you may be going through, if you're relying on the Spirit, then His fruit is being brought forth in your life. The Holy Spirit through His given gifts is producing His acceptable fruit. Gifts from the Lord have holy spores of transformation attached to them. They may not always feel good, but they often dislodge someone from where they have been to where He wants them to be.

I encouraged my downcast friend, regarding his move, that God's Word was shaping him in order to make him capable of its fulfillment. When I shared the same scripture with him in a different translation, below, he began to cry.

> He had already sent a man ahead of his people to Egypt;
> it was Joseph, who was sold as a slave.
> His feet were bruised by strong shackles
> and his soul was held by iron.
> God's promise to Joseph purged his character
> *until it was time* for his dreams to come true.
>
> (Ps. 105:17–19 TPT, MY EMPHASIS)

The word that you release, the healing you declare, the gifts you activate have more than a temporal result. Don't get me wrong, wisdom is needed, healing is needed, miracles need to happen. But there is an eternal benefit as your soul is nourished with nutrients that supercharge your growth in God. The fruit of the Spirit will rise out of the ashes of despair. You are on the back nine being developed as a champion. You will finish the course and finish strong. Jesus is waiting at the clubhouse to welcome you!

Spiritual gifts are not natural gifts. Natural gifts are given to you at natural birth. Spiritual gifts are given at spiritual birth. Many Christians will go through life not knowing nor discovering the great riches given to them in Jesus Christ. You are gifted for the profit of all.

A quick look at the disciples Jesus selected will indicate that He was looking ultimately for strength of heart rather than maturity.

Over time, maturity would come from actually being with and doing ministry with Jesus. The release of gifts from the Spirit is almost like becoming an apprentice for Christlikeness. Arguably, we can say that the three years the disciples were with Jesus were their front nine.

Even up until Pentecost, they were still dealing with character flaws. Limited understanding of the full impact of the freedom of Pentecost continued in the prejudice toward widows (Acts 6), and hesitations about Cornelius (Acts 10). My point is that they were still maturing even when serving in the most prominent roles of the early church. They were not perfect. There were probably many messes, partly because there was only one requirement: obedience.

MYSTERY TO MASTERY

If you're obedient in surrendering your heart to God, then He will use you. When I was ten years old, relatively new to the faith, I began to experiment with the gifts of the Spirit. I had been filled with the Spirit but was obviously a novice. One Sunday night when I sensed the Spirit moving within, I stood in church and belted out a prophetic word that stunned the crowd. It wasn't because of the awesomeness of the word but the age of the deliverer. To the credit of my church, they never put an age limit on me, and I continued to grow.

The gifting can transform you. The anointing can teach you. The faith can expand your sphere. It can bring a deeper relationship because you change in the presence of God.

For the disciples, Pentecost seemed to be the "turn" at the golf course, the transition from the front nine to the back nine. They were still carrying the power of the front nine but were being loosened up to play a strong back nine. As any strong golfer will tell you, the back nine requires strength, character, and skill. The second half of the round in golf is about finishing well. For believers, the back nine is about being more established, secure, healed, and faithful. In reference to the fruit of the Spirit, the back nine becomes the harvest that naturally grows out of the experience of the front nine, the gifts. You jump in and move in the gifts only to be fashioned into the image of Jesus, thus bearing the fruit of the Spirit.

This progressive life that takes us from glory to glory will also take us from mystery to mastery. God's will is for us to grow up in Him: "Solid food belongs to those who are of full age, that is, those who by reason of use have their senses exercised to discern both good and evil" (Heb. 5:14). The "reason of use" creates greater discernment. Use is powerful. Activating the Holy Spirit and unleashing Him in your life will transform you in every way. God calls us to practice His gifts, and the performing of them will actually change us while glorifying God.

GET A GRIP

My golf game was transformed by one comment by an elderly man. His words would become an illustration about wisdom for a key moment. His one comment took ten strokes off my game almost instantly. I had hit a wall for years, never breaking certain barriers. Then one day, when my wife and I arrived at the course, we were told that we would have to form a foursome with another couple. Initially, I wasn't excited about that. It was my day off, and I couldn't imagine spending time making small talk with people I didn't know. With little choice, however, we met the elderly couple in our arranged foursome and began to play.

Several holes in, I was up standing at the tee when I noticed the older man had slipped around to my right and was watching my swing. Distracted and a bit annoyed, I turned to him and asked if everything was all right. He said, "I think I might be able to help you."

I really was not in the mood for instruction, but as a courtesy, I said, "Sure, thanks." He then told me the secret of the "long thumb," demonstrating an awkward grip for me to try when I hit the ball. Growing even more aggravated at his uninvited instruction, I did as instructed just to get through it. Expecting nothing, I proceeded to hit the longest and straightest ball of the day! The more I used my long-thumb grip, the better I got. That summer I trimmed ten strokes off of my game.

Here's my point: Moving in faith to use your gifts can feel awkward. Over time, though, it starts to feel natural, and a new level of maturity comes upon you. Not only did my game improve, but my character was adjusted. His word of wisdom improved my golf game, while God used it to bear spiritual fruit.

THE MASTER'S TOURNAMENT

Once in the habit of sharing your gifts, you can then see God at work in numerous and various ways. My personal gifts have been mainly in the revelatory sector of the gifts. I tend to easily discern and speak knowledge, wisdom, or the prophetic to everyone around me. Sometimes it is with intent, and other times it is seemingly by accident. When I release my spiritual gifts to others, I'm blessed by giving. It is the law of reciprocity. Whatever you sow, you will reap. If you sow into others the good things of God, you will also reap the same. The more I prophesy, the more I understand and receive about myself.

In fact, the more I move in spiritual gifts, the more I have the opportunity to bear the fruit of the Spirit. The Bible says to "cast your bread upon the waters, for you will find it after many days" (Eccl. 11:1). What the tide takes out, it will bring back to you. My growth in the Lord over the years is a combination of studying His Word and moving in His Spirit.

Part of your destiny will be determined by your openness to God and His gifts to you. There will be moments when you don't understand the what or why or when of this world. But God provides all you need through His gifts. Information or power from heaven can change everything. Your submission to a life of being used by God can create a world of change in your heart.

The fruit of the Spirit in Galatians is produced by walking in the Spirit. Galatians 5 says that if you "walk in the Spirit…you will not fulfill the lust of the flesh" (v. 16). We see a contrast of the works of the flesh and the fruit of the Spirit. We can infer that no matter which you choose, they both bear fruit—albeit very different kinds of fruit!

Referring to fleshly fruit, Paul listed seventeen or more, while identifying nine fruit of the Spirit. Also, note that *fruit* refers to an entire harvest as well as to individual specific fruit within the harvest. The fruit of walking in the Spirit brings love, joy, peace, long-suffering, kindness, goodness, faithfulness, gentleness, and self-control. There is a direct correlation. God gives His gifts to the imperfect to move us to the fruit of the Perfect, Jesus Christ Himself.

Scripture indicates that a life in the Spirit, which means a life that manifests the spiritual gifts, will bring about behavior changes. God gives us the Spirit to manifest the Spirit so we can become like the Lord Jesus. Your yielding to His gifts will bring the fruit that only God can give. Your action to respond to God brings attitudinal shifts. "As you yield freely and fully to the dynamic life and power of the Holy Spirit, you will abandon the cravings of your self-life" (Gal. 5:16 TPT).

No matter where you may be in your journey of faith, you can put down even deeper roots in the Spirit and bear more fruit. Use what He has freely given you. Do not wait to become perfect. Let Him move you toward the Perfect One. Surrender your gifts and watch God produce fruit. Utilizing your front nine to produce amazing results on your back nine, God will show you how to win the Master's tournament!

YOUR VIEW FROM HERE

Your spiritual gifts were not given for your own benefit but for the benefit of others, just as other people were given gifts for your benefit.
—RICK WARREN

1. Describe your understanding of the relationship between the gifts of the Spirit and the fruit of the Spirit. Instead of the game of golf, what would you compare them to? Why?

2. When have you witnessed the transformation of your spiritual gifting into spiritual harvest? How has God used you lately to plant seed in the lives of others? What fruit is presently growing in their lives? And in yours?

3. Find a small group of people committed to the practice of spiritual gifts. Get to know them and learn from one another. Move toward what God has created you to be, and then grow in maturity by spiritual service to one another. Using your spiritual gifts, watch and see how the Lord will use spiritual seed to reap His fruitful harvest in your life—and in the lives of those around you.

For as the body is one and has many members, but all the members of that one body, being many, are one body, so also is Christ.
—1 CORINTHIANS 12:12

CHAPTER 13

LONGITUDE AND LATITUDE

Finding Your Prophetic Sweet Spot

A man's gift makes room for him,
and brings him before great men.
—PROVERBS 18:16

Energy and persistence conquer all things.
—BEN FRANKLIN

My daughter Lauren spent fifteen years after high school experiencing travel, studying personal interests, and exploring a variety of jobs. She ended up earning a degree and getting married but still had no sense of a career direction. Soon, though, she realized she loved helping people find places to rent. Something about the fulfillment of others' dreams also fulfilled hers. As a result of her discovery, she studied and received her Realtor's license.

Upon being hired, she carved out a path that was slightly different from other traditional real estate agents. Her savvy use of social media advertising and fluid work style rocketed her into a successful first year, becoming agent of the month several times, thanks to producing multimillion-dollar sales. She is now building a team for long-term growth. Her clients have said they like that she isn't a traditional pushy salesperson and that she clearly loves what she does.

Basically, my daughter has found her sweet spot.

SWEET SUCCESS

It's the sound of a baseball bat, announcing that this ball is heading for the fence. It's that easy swing of a golf club, magically lifting the ball to its maximum destination. It's that place on the tennis racket, shooting your serve with ferocity and velocity. Crossing into many sectors, a sweet spot opens the way for ultimate performance and success.

Nobody totally knows where the term "sweet spot" originated. Some argue that it began in the oil industry, referring to holes drilled in hopes of striking oil. The term has been popularized in many sports, including baseball, tennis, and golf. Just as in playing these games, finding the sweet spot can be a matter of inches or fractions thereof. A simple adjustment to where you are and what you do can open a sweet spot in your life. Sweet spots create greater accuracy, generate more power, and yield longer results. They demonstrate that more strength and thought doesn't solve all problems. A sweet spot opens a portal between heaven and earth, unleashing a mysterious flow of fulfilled potential.

As a committed follower of Jesus, I'm in constant pursuit of the nuanced sweet spot in my spiritual life. As stewards of this life God has given us, we're called to blossom and produce great fruit. We're devoted to using His spiritual gifts to produce the fruit of the Spirit. In the process, we often discover the greatest joy, peace, and fulfillment. Being activated to our maximum capacity brings great satisfaction. Scripture's wisdom says, "The path of the just is like the shining sun, that shines ever brighter unto the perfect day" (Prov. 4:18).

Your sweet spot is the pivot point for maximum benefit. Everyone has a sweet spot in their destiny that is activated when three elements converge: personal currencies, passions, and choice design. Blending these ingredients results in the discovery of your God-given self. Unleashing what God placed inside you and learning through hard-won experience, you discover what He has created you to do in this life.

BURIED TREASURE

Discovering your sweet spot is not a perfect science—or, as one of my favorite books, *Designing Your Life*, expresses it, "There is no dream job. No unicorns. No free lunch."[1] Accepting that there's no magic formula or direct path to your sweet spot removes the pressure to crack life's code and get it right the first time. You're free to explore the imperfect, balancing this life outside the garden of Eden where we survive by the sweat of our brow with the kingdom of God growing inside us like a heavenly garden. Occasionally, we experience certain times and places where heaven meets earth, and we glimpse what heaven is like. Those moments open our eyes to the ultimate sweet spot. They reveal channels of divine flow, carrying us on a current we can often enjoy for extended periods of time.

When these three components—currencies, passions, and a healthy construct for decision-making—are combined, they produce movement. In chapter 8 we've already focused on what's required to make good decisions, so here we'll explore currencies and passions. They are often the raw material God uses to transform us into the architects of His greatest accomplishments in our lives. Currencies and passions can function like longitude and latitude to help you find God's treasure buried within you.

By this point, you know how much I like charts to help visualize various concepts, so let's look at the Sweet Spot Chart. When you get your three circles fired up, you not only move toward opportunities, but they are also magnetically attracted to you. The spiritual movement in your life attracts others to you. All employers love people with positive energy who have direction and purpose in their lives. They want to employ those people who are good decision makers and problem solvers. Often, unexpected opportunities will show up if you just keep being faithful to what God has put in your hand.

HAND IT TO GOD

As we consider the concept of personal currency, I can't think of a better example than Moses. One of the greatest figures of the Bible, he was prepared and called by God for a special task. When God initiated contact with him, Moses was shepherding in a remote desert wilderness and suddenly a burning bush demanded his attention (Ex. 3). The voice of God came out of the bush and challenged Moses to a task that defined who he was and would become. Prior to that moment, Moses had been outside his sweet spot. He was, in fact, hiding from his destiny. He had drifted so far from his destiny that his personal view of self was damaged and distorted.

At first, Moses protested, "Who am I that I should go to Pharaoh, and that I should bring the children of Israel out of Egypt?" (v. 11). Recall from Exodus 2, Moses was raised as royalty, the adopted son of Pharaoh's daughter, after being set afloat in a reed basket on the river. His mother knew God wanted her son to escape the mass slaughter of baby boys commanded by Pharaoh, becoming fearful as Hebrews began to outnumber Egyptians. Consequently, Moses should have been confident of his ability and strength of character; he was special and had been spared. But as an adult, he had lashed out in anger and killed an Egyptian overseer who had been mistreating a Jewish slave. Moses had to flee for his life and ended up hiding in the desert. God was calling him back into the mess he had run away from.

After God addressed Moses' initial excuses, the fearful shepherd said, "But suppose they will not believe me or listen to my voice; suppose they say, 'The LORD has not appeared to you'" (4:1).

God responded by asking, "What is that in your hand?" (v. 2). Of course, the Lord already knew what was in Moses' hand, but He called attention to the rod in the shepherd's grasp to make His point. God told Moses to throw down his rod, and when he did, it transformed into a snake. When God told him to pick up the snake by its tail, it returned to being his rod.

The Lord used what Moses already had in his hand to demonstrate how God could use it. Moses already had all he needed to fulfill the divine purpose to which he was called. Similarly, any skill or tool in our possession can be transformed into an agent of God's power for His purposes. Like lightning rods for spiritual empowerment, these conduits become charged by the Spirit and change our life and the lives of others. They are the currencies God gives us to spend, backed up by His heavenly riches, as we advance His kingdom on earth.

As a member of an oppressed minority, Moses knew what it was to be enslaved and despised. As an adopted son of Egyptian royalty, he also knew what it was to have privilege and receive the best education. He knew what it was to exert power over another and to feel powerless as a result of his impulsive action. Forty years later, he stood before the burning bush, and God asked what was in his hand. God had been preparing Moses throughout all the ups and downs of his life.

The same is true for you and me. God uses who we are. He uses your past. He uses what is in your hands. Just as God transformed something ordinary and mundane, a shepherd's staff, into a tool for negotiation and warfare, He still empowers us today. Our ordinary becomes extraordinary through the power of God in us. He uses whatever is in our hand to become something dangerously alive.

God loves to use people where they are, what they have, and who they know. While He can certainly create something out of nothing, we also see a biblical pattern showing that He loves to transform our little into His great. We see that God gives "beauty for ashes, the oil of joy for mourning, the garment of praise for the spirit of heaviness" (Isa. 61:3). A little boy's lunch of bread and fish feeds multitudes. Water becomes wine.

Your life has meaning, even if it has been full of wrong choices and painful consequences. God takes the crumbs and bakes a cake. God loves to restore, rebuild, and recreate broken lives. He is the Redeemer. The very thing that represents years of pain and difficulty may become the tool that He uses to deliver multitudes. The Lord has fashioned you. He has prepared you. He knows your weakness.

We wait for God to move on our behalf, and He simply says, "What is that in your hand?" What does God have in your hand right now? What transformational power might there be if you accept His calling and gifting?

A BRANCH BLOSSOMS

Moses wasn't the only one in Scripture with a currency that God transformed. The prophet Jeremiah began to glimpse his God-breathed destiny when he was still a youth. God asked him, "What do you see?" to which the young Jeremiah responded, "I see a branch of an almond tree" (Jer. 1:11). The almond branch was believed to be the symbol of potential fulfilled, since it was among the first to blossom each spring. God used what was natural and readily available to prophesy about the future. This appears to be a common practice in the way God often communicates. Using the almond branch, God began training Jeremiah and preparing him for his destiny.

Similarly, we see in Genesis 39–47 how God used the skills of administration in Joseph to save not only his own life or the lives of his family but millions of lives—basically the known world. Joseph obviously had leadership and organizational skills that caused him to excel everywhere he went, even in difficult situations. While serving as a slave to an Egyptian official named Potiphar, Joseph became head of his master's household thanks to his skills and the Lord's favor. It didn't take long, however, before false accusations from Potiphar's wife sent Joseph to prison.

Once again, the favor of God and his personal skills enabled Joseph to rise to a position of leadership. From there, his ability to interpret dreams became the catalyst for his release—both from prison and from the limitations of his past. After successfully interpreting Pharaoh's dream, Joseph was promoted to be second-in-command in all of ancient Egypt. He implemented a strategy including tactical structures that saved all of Egypt while bringing great wealth and power into his sovereign's country.

His God-given ability not only saved a nation but served as the foundation for the restoration of his own broken family relationships. The Lord worked all things together for Joseph's good and blessed a nation at the same time. As Joseph told his brothers, "But as for you, you meant evil against me; but God meant it for good, in order to bring it about as it is this day, to save many people alive" (Gen. 50:20).

FINDING YOUR SWEET SPOT

What does God want you to use as tools for finding your sweet spot and building His kingdom?

INVEST YOUR CURRENCY

What's in your life right now that God wants to use as the currency of your destiny? While the items and elements are as personal and unique as a fingerprint, let's consider seven commodities that often serve as currency to receive God's power in our lives as we find our sweet spots:

Time. Our days are numbered. Our time on earth can be heavy with value or pass like dust in the wind. It can be used to further your education, provide rest from weariness, overcome a challenge, or time can be wasted on an aimless lifestyle of narcissistic pleasure and purposeless gain. You can never recover time lost. Your time is constantly being spent, moment by moment, hour by hour, day by day. Without a doubt, time is the most important currency of all.

Energy. Energy's currency increases in value the older you get. In your twenties, you anticipate feeling the way you do then for the rest of your life. But as you age, you realize your energy level is neither stable nor infinite. Life tempers your energy. Poor health can quickly drain you of this currency. Depression can nuke your drive and immobilize your divine potential. On the other hand, a healthy lifestyle can raise the odds for you to sustain your strength, but this, too, can change in the blink of an eye. Energy must be used effectively while you have it.

Money. Money may be the most obvious destiny currency. How you use your money is probably one of the greatest factors in your quality of life. Poor management can lead to robbed destinies. Debt can affect you financially, emotionally, and physically. The burden of debt makes you rigid and earthbound. You become a slave. Financial freedom and living within your means add wings to your destiny and enable you to be nimble, fluid, flexible, and free. You cannot serve God and money. Debt changes the structure of your life into servitude to money. Use and invest it wisely!

Skills. You can exert the most control over this particular currency. Everyone can increase skill levels. Skills are a currency that can be increased. You may be born with talent, but skills are acquired and developed. Experience and training provide the most pliable and manageable currency that you have. Basic skills needed for life include communication, memory, human relations, management of money, time, and so on. Skills take time to develop. Major skills may necessitate extended education, certification, or tenure. Everyone needs something they are good at, and preferably something that can also create a real income.

Talents and Gifts. Everyone has talents. They may be unrecognized or undeveloped, but they are there. Some talents are more obvious, particularly those of the arts. Without any formal training or preparation, some people just shine at what they do. It doesn't seem fair at times, and truth is, sometimes it isn't. Some people do have it easier than others. Let's get over it and get on with finding what our talent is. Friends, family, and associates can help you discover your core talents—so ask them.

History. While it may sound strange, your history is a currency. Even a checkered past can become the launching pad for your greatness. Just as we can see in the lives of Moses and Joseph, a painful past can become the proving ground for God's power to unlock our potential. Trusting the Lord, you can use your past to learn and grow—or you can pull away from Him and allow your old wounds to fester. As the old saying goes, "You can get bitter or better." Honest assessment of your history can help you discover where your strengths have appeared and where weaknesses have abounded.

Too often, history hinders us. It negatively shapes our view of self and robs us of our destiny. Sometimes the trauma of the past is so overwhelming that it immobilizes your potential—but only as long as you allow it to do so. God has designed you to extend your soul in dark times of pain and reap a harvest of light and joy. Learning to step out of your own pain, even when you do not feel like it, strangely unlocks your own personal destiny. See your history as a unique weaving of God's grace that will be used in your destiny fulfillment. He did not cause your pain, but He will not waste it. Your earthly pain can become your heavenly gain.

Revelation. The final currency is our ability to access heaven. Multiple Bible stories recount destiny shifts as people avail the ability to access the unknown and bring its power into the known. Daniel was a slave. At the right moment he downloaded special understanding from heaven that saved his life and promoted him to favor. The use of heaven's secrets can change your landscape and accelerate your destiny. Your ability to hear from God, even in the most traumatic circumstances, will spare future pain and create new opportunities for advancement in knowledge and position.

What's in your hand? Let God use what you already possess to lead you to freedom and fulfillment. Let His power transform your pain into purpose.

UNLEASH YOUR PASSION

In addition to currency, passion provides the other major component for finding your sweet spot. It's your fuel for advancement. What gets you up in the morning? What stirs your soul? Sometimes when we think of passion, we move toward the negative example of unbridled passions. But our God-given passions should command our attention.

IDENTIFY YOUR MOTIVATION

In truth, you are being motivated by something greater within you. What are the components that motivate you and keep you moving even in the midst of adversity?

God wants to use our passions to fulfill our divine purpose. The Bible says, "Whatever you do, do it heartily, as to the Lord and not to men" (Col. 3:23). Here, the word *heartily* is from the Greek and literally means "from the soul." Our soul is the seedbed of passion. It creates the energy that moves you toward your destiny. Men and women of God have frequently moved forward by natural and spiritual passion. David was driven with a passion to restore the place of God's presence. Nehemiah was moved by the difficulties in Jerusalem. Ruth was motivated by her concern and love for Naomi.

ASK YOURSELF KEY QUESTIONS

Over the years, I've used three questions to help people assess their life passions:

- If you knew you would succeed at whatever you did, what would you attempt?
- If you had a hundred million dollars in the bank, what would you do with the rest of your life?
- If you knew you had only six months left to live, how would you spend your time?

While these questions are more temporally focused, they hold keys to unlocking what you care most about and are called to do in this life. I encourage you to set aside time and pray. Ask the Lord to open your understanding as you ponder your life. These diagnostic questions will open your thinking and get you focused on priorities that are most important to you.

If those three questions seem too big or too challenging to answer, then use these additional questions below to unlock your passion and pursue your sweet spot:

What tasks energize me?

What people would I most like to help me?

What are three things I have felt passionate about in the past?

What would others say I'm passionate about?

What do I love to spend money on?

What do the prophetic words spoken over me reveal?

Who, what, and where are the people, places, and things that stir my soul?

You get the idea. Once you discover what you really want to invest your time and energy in, then you dig deeper. Ask the *why* question. Why would you quit your job and travel the world? Why would you buy houses for all of your relatives? Why would you write a book?

Do some assessment and then get someone to lay hands on you and pray. Seek the fire of the Holy Spirit to burn away what's holding you back. When the disciples received the Holy Spirit, there was an energy that caused them to stand up and act. They became passionate about what God wanted. They had potential in them before but needed a stirring. Once stirred, they could never be shaken!

You may be stuck in a career that feels like a dead end, but the fire of God can change your environment and accelerate you toward a sweet spot that opens new doors. If you have no idea what to do, get busy with what God has already told you to do and see what emerges.

Sometimes we live in a fantasy that has been propped up by well-meaning encouragers and even by prophetic words over our lives. We borrow emotionally from that potential without really living it out. Our Christian lives become an avatar of the exploits of what we may do yet escape the reality of our current responsibilities. The future is not guaranteed for anyone. All we have is in the present.

All you have is what's in your hand. Do what is before you and watch God expand your horizons. Get fired up about living in your sweet spot. Nations may be waiting for you to discover what God has already given you. Do the hard work of self-discovery in order to align with the prophetic design over your life. With the Holy Spirit as your Guide, your sweet spot is just ahead!

YOUR VIEW FROM HERE

Some painters transform the sun into a yellow spot, others transform a yellow spot into the sun.

—Pablo Picasso

1. Think about times in your life when you were in your sweet spot. What do those times have in common? What can you do to facilitate more opportunities for enjoying what God created you to do?

2. When have you seen God use what was in your hand in order to reveal His power or further His kingdom? What were the circumstances? How did it feel at the time? What present currency is in your life that you sense He wants to use?

3. After spending a few moments in prayer seeking the Spirit's guidance, go back to the big three diagnostic questions to uncover what you're most passionate about. Reflect on how you would answer each one and then write your answer, describing in a brief paragraph why you answered this way. What do all three of your answers have in common? What direction are they

pointing in? What do you need to do to align your life
with this direction?

You came near when I called you, and you said, "Do
not fear." You, Lord, took up my case; you redeemed
my life.

—LAMENTATIONS 3:57–58 NIV

CHAPTER 14

UNEXPECTED TURBULENCE

Gaining Perspective Above Your Pain

Now no chastening seems to be joyful for the
present, but painful; nevertheless, afterward it
yields the peaceable fruit of righteousness to those
who have been trained by it.

—HEBREWS 12:11

There are two types of pain in this world: pain
that hurts you, and pain that changes you.

—UNKNOWN

On a recent trip to Italy, my wife, Cindy, and I were visiting
a beautiful Tuscan hill town when she experienced severe
pain and numbness in her leg. We were right in the middle of our
much-anticipated, three-week journey of rest and renewal when this

unexpected pain interrupted our joyful excursion. There's never a good time to suffer health problems, but they're especially unwelcomed when you're traveling.

We made our way into Pisa and settled into an ER waiting room for five hours. Compounding our concern for Cindy's leg was our awareness of the added complications of a foreign language and cultural differences. Eventually, an English-speaking doctor treated her, showing us great kindness and humor. He told me that Italy has the best health-care system in the world, to which I replied, "Well, today you do!" After conducting several tests, this doctor assured us that Cindy's ailment was not deep vein thrombosis and released her. Her pain began dissipating and soon disappeared without recurring again.

Relieved and exhausted from our medical detour, we thought, *What a waste of time!* But then as we continued imagining the possibilities we had been spared, we became mindful of life's fragility. Our plans could be interrupted at any time. In the book of James we're reminded that "you do not know what will happen tomorrow. For what is your life? It is even a vapor that appears for a little time and then vanishes away" (4:14). Pain's intrusion reminded us that every journey has bumps in the road. Everything in life can change in a moment's notice.

LOST AND FOUND

There's no way around it—pain hurts! Unfortunately, although we are on the other side of the cross, we are on this side of heaven. Pain will find its way to you, or you might even create it yourself. Every life has its share of hardships. No one wants them, but they're nevertheless part of our journey. So the question becomes, how will we handle pain when it comes? Will we allow pain to derail us from our destination? Or will it lead us to discover a deeper sense of God's love and power within us?

Periodically, it profits us to be reminded that life is full of pain and disappointment. We mindlessly make wrong turns, end up in places that were not our choice, and at times brazenly forge a direction that does not reflect our past values or experiences. In other words, we get lost.

When we stray, we can find comfort knowing God never abandons us. Jesus gives us comfort in His three related parables about a missing sheep, a lost coin, and a prodigal son (Luke 15). The sheep just made a wrong turn wandering, the coin had no choice, and the son made an eye-opening wrong choice. The first two were pursued by those responsible for their care—the good shepherd and the woman who lost the coin. In the third parable, the loving father waited on the wayward son.

Some pain needs rescuing, and some pain needs self-awareness and correction. Some pain requires the rescue of others, and some pain forces you to come to your senses and return home to God's waiting embrace. Despite how random, unfair, and arbitrary it may feel to you, your pain always has a lesson attached to it. The wise will search it out.

Regardless of the source of your pain, you always face an opportunity for a positive or negative response. On our Italian vacation, my wife and I first felt frustrated and disappointed before being tremendously thankful that nothing serious was wrong with her. We also quickly realized how this painful experience established a resolve to more deeply enjoy our time remaining.

Tomorrow is not promised, so we must choose to live every day as if it were our last. While it has become cliché, this truth still contains great biblical wisdom. Our life is indeed a vapor. I've attempted to live out this principle most of my adult life. Every time something comes upon me that is painful, I accept the potential of earthly consequences and then move forward from there. I cannot control tomorrow, just this present moment.

Dale Carnegie, the famed self-improvement guru of the early twentieth century, advised, "If someone hands you a lemon, make a lemonade."[1] This, too, may sound cliché but remains true nonetheless. Sometimes you have to revise your plan and change your attitude to fit a preferred future. You will have to squeeze the sour moments of pain until something sweet comes from them. The psalms offer insight on making this kind of lemonade:

> Blessed is the man whose strength is in You,
> Whose heart is set on pilgrimage.
> As they pass through the Valley of Baca,
> They make it a spring;
> The rain also covers it with pools.
> They go from strength to strength;
> Each one appears before God in Zion.
>
> (Ps. 84:5–7)

Like the pilgrim in this passage, our hearts are set on something better in God, but we come upon the Valley of Baca, a place similar to the "valley of the shadow of death" (Ps. 23:4). Valleys were ancient places of vulnerability, which explains the importance of high places. This low point is that place of pain, suffering, doubt, fear, and lack of control. In those low, vulnerable places on your journey, God is with you. In fact, Psalm 23 promises that the Lord will be with you and has gone ahead to prepare a table in the midst of your enemies (v. 5).

Baca literally means "weeping," so it is the valley of our greatest anguish, the place we must cross as we journey toward our God-given destiny. The psalmist does not define what has caused the weeping, but there is a sense of its inevitably for those on a pilgrimage.

Curiously enough, though, for those who know the Lord, these tears transform the valley into a spring (Ps. 84:6). The pain you encounter in your life can become a place of refreshment, restoring life just as the rain does, from "strength to strength" (v. 7).

Our most difficult times are transformed into fertile soil for new growth. Our tears in one season become the rain watering the seeds God has planted within us for the next. The valleys in our life are necessary, providing life-altering and soul-shaping moments that forever change our trajectory. As we seek God, our pain is converted into a wellspring of joy. Our greatest losses in life can reveal a fresh understanding of what matters most.

Pain has to be managed. It has to be reframed. It has to serve our mission and our destination. The writer of Hebrews wrote an entire chapter, often called "The Hall of Faith," featuring a historical list of people who made wrong turns, encountered much pain, but then experienced God's transformative power. They became champions of faith! Their example of faithfulness in the face of pain encourages me.

NO PAIN, NO GAIN

Today's culture doesn't see great benefit to pain, unless in reference to sports. We all seem to understand that to be a great athlete you must experience pain, delay, and disappointment in your desire to rise as a champion. Even in business, there is what Malcolm Gladwell, author of *Outliers*, calls the "10,000-hour rule." His theory is, to become world class in any field requires at least 10,000 hours of practice. Whether the number is exact, clearly there's an enormous commitment to continual practice that yields the experience required for mastery. Over the course of so much practice, there are inevitably sprained muscles, disappointing outcomes, broken strings, bankrupt businesses, and crushing betrayals.

As Christians, sometimes we believe that because God is good and loving, we will never experience anything painful. This notion is not based in biblical, natural, or realistic thinking. The rain falls on the just and the unjust and sometimes falls unjustly on the just!

Western Christianity has also been gripped by erroneous thinking that our pilgrimage should always be blissful, idyllic, and predictable. Just as we each carefully script and photoshop our social media to present the best possible viewing, we want to look as if we have the best life possible. In reality, drug addiction and suicides soar in a culture that has greater connectivity than ever yet lacks true intimacy. Our pain is real and more alive than ever just beneath the surface, just beyond our latest status pic. The church might fare better if we were known as a house of pain, filled with broken people who are dependent on a loving God. Jesus has the ability to turn our mourning into dancing, our ashes into beauty, and depression into praise.

Contrary to modern thinking, life is pocked with doubt, fear, terror, instability, and pain. Jesus Himself had a moment of request when He pleaded, "Father, if it is Your will, take this cup away from Me" (Luke 22:42). His pain was great but accepted as part of life on this side of heaven. Christ immediately restated His request by conceding, "Nevertheless not My will, but Yours, be done." He was willing to submit, although His preference was to avoid the pain ahead of Him.

Did Jesus have an understanding that God the Father was saying no to Him? Was this painful? He prayed in agony, and we're told that His sweat became great drops of blood (v. 44). Adding insult to agony, when He went to see His disciples in the greatest hour of need, they were sleeping (v. 45). Even for the Son of God, pain remained part of the pilgrimage toward God. Why would we expect to avoid what Christ Himself endured on our behalf?

REVENGE OR REDEMPTION

Even as you experience pain on many levels, you can learn to turn your suffering into opportunities for growing closer to God and for refining your character for your ultimate destiny. As we've seen in the lives of Joseph and so many others in the Bible, what others intended for evil, God transformed and used for good. The very dream that God gave Joseph ironically produced the greatest pain in his life. That pain became the tool in the hands of a loving God that carved out the requisite capacity for Joseph's ultimate role. The pain was used to hew him out, with less of him and more of God.

Joseph famously went from enjoying his privileged status as his father's favorite into a pit of rejection from his brothers. Sold into slavery, he finally emerged again, only to be sexually harassed and falsely accused. This event put him into prison. From the time of his brothers' betrayal until he ruled beneath Pharaoh in Egypt, Joseph endured thirteen years of agony. For more than a decade, he never gave up faith in God and hope for the future.

Eventually, Joseph's dream was fulfilled as he stood in lordship over his brothers with their lives in his hands. The moment of reciprocity was upon him. All his long-simmering pain boiled over into a moment with perfect potential for revenge. No one would blame him—we might even root for him to even the score after such a devastating rejection. Yet, the pain worked something deeper in this man. Joseph wept and could forgive his brothers because he had seen what God had done despite their betrayal of him.

Your pain can lead to revenge or redemption.

God's love is transcendent. When we experience it, His love overpowers our anger, squelches the broken memories, heals lingering wounds, and restores our souls. Love is the chief currency of heaven. Love will never fail. Perfect love casts out fear. God is the essence of love. God is love.

God doesn't guarantee you a life free from pain. He does give you love. Love covers a multitude of sins when you miss the mark. Love is an emancipator. It frees you even in the midst of your pain. God's passion is the crafting of a demonstration of love that affects generations. Jesus said, "A new commandment I give to you, that you love one another; as I have loved you, that you also love one another. By this all will know that you are My disciples, if you have love for one another" (John 13:34–35).

HELLO, NEIGHBOR

It's not easy to love others, especially when we've not been loved well ourselves. But our wounds don't let us off the hook. God calls us to trust Him and move forward in using our gifts to bear fruit all the same. He knows your testimony becomes all the more powerful and points back to Him when you're able to transcend your pain and love with purpose.

One of my favorite examples of this kind of love emerges from a surprising source. Many Americans either grew up watching *Mr. Rogers' Neighborhood* or were parents allowing their children to do so. Fred Rogers was an even-keeled man with a heart for children despite the pain of his own childhood. In the documentary of his life *Won't You Be My Neighbor?* we learn that he spent much of his childhood battling various illnesses, often confined to bed. In that lonely place of pain and separation, his imagination began to take off. The suffering that could have emotionally crippled so many became a launching pad for an imagination that touched millions of children's lives.

Fred Rogers developed a keen sense of reading people and adapting his communication accordingly. As a minister sent out by his denomination, he became a missionary in the relatively new world of television. Considering the elements that made so many other TV shows successful at the time, Fred's show did the exact opposite. The transcendent love of Mr. Rogers mattered in the 1960s, and it matters now. He allowed his brokenness to better serve others, and he became an icon of gentleness, kindness, and good humor for several generations.

I'm firmly convinced that Mr. Rogers's success over three decades was due to his deep understanding of the love of God. His TV neighborhood was a place where everyone practiced loving their neighbors as themselves. He created a safe place to explore and explain weighty, complicated issues such as war, divorce, anger, and racism to children. He removed fear and brought peace, even to the point of teaching children to pause, observe, and be silent. He once put an egg timer on for one minute to see how long a minute was. That one minute of dead airspace demonstrated the calmness of a life of love and peace. Sometimes silence speaks more than the incessant sounds and voices of current culture. He was brilliant in a childlike way.

The documentary shows a 1960s news clip of white people pouring chlorine into a public pool to cleanse it from black children who were joyfully swimming. While our country struggled with accepting civil rights for all people regardless of race, Mr. Rogers welcomed a new cast member, Officer Clemmons, to his show. Having a black actor portray a policeman on television was groundbreaking, but Fred Rogers didn't stop there. He treated Officer Clemmons with the same respect and kindness as he did everyone else.

In one memorable episode, Mr. Rogers invited Officer Clemmons into his house to wash his feet in a small tub and cool down from the summer heat. The policeman hesitated because he didn't have a towel, but Mr. Rogers assured his friend that they could share his towel. That was radical at the time! Scenes like this taught children to love regardless of color. That is transcending love. Mr. Rogers served as a conduit of the supernatural power of God's love to shape a generation. Rather than camp in the painful reality of his past, he used it to improve the future for others. He knew that only love heals pain.

HOT AND COLD

Andy Andrews, the well-known storyteller and author of the book *The Noticer* and many others, calls the choice to choose love over pain the "joyful decision." It's the decision in the midst of life's most excruciating events to create a new narrative, a supernatural one. Your pain can define you in positive ways. You can choose to create a different story. Andrews wrote in *The Seven Decisions*, "Our very lives are fashioned by choice. First we make choices. Then our choices make us."[2]

It is easy for pain to kill love and put out your fire of passion. Love can grow cold as life has a way of cooling down the embers. Unexpected trauma or physical health issues can chill a life full of passion and dreams. Speaking about the end times, Jesus declared, "The love of many will grow cold" (Matt. 24:12). The fires of love have to be tended even in difficult times.

King David discovered this truth. Although known as a man after God's own heart (Acts 13:22), the shepherd-king endured a cooling period in his life. It happened in his ascendency to the throne as he awaited the fulfillment of the prophetic anointing on his life. Known for his passion and spiritual fervor, David lost his zeal even as he gained rank, wealth, and royal title. He was known for his exploits yet got careless and moved away from God and from the life God had called him to live.

As his spiritual focus blurred, David walked into a trap at a weak moment. In the 2 Samuel 11 account, David, strolling on his rooftop one sleepless night, gazed at Bathsheba bathing and was self-seduced. Her husband, Uriah, was at war in service to David's army while the king slept with his soldier's wife. David's sin didn't stop there. After finding out that Bathsheba was pregnant, the king called her husband home in an attempted cover-up, hoping the man would sleep with his wife and later assume her child was his own. Uriah, however, was too committed to his king and God to do such a thing. So David got the soldier drunk in hopes of releasing the man's reservations, which failed as well when Uriah fell asleep.

Then David plotted with his general to push Uriah into the heat of the battle on the front line. There Uriah was killed, and David took the dead man's wife as his own. All of David's deceptive schemes might have remained hidden except for the divine revelation given to Nathan, God's prophet. Nathan approached David and told a story of a rich man and a poor man. The rich man had everything and the poor man had only one lamb, the equivalent to a family pet. Receiving a guest, the rich man went and killed the poor man's sheep to fill his table. Hearing Nathan's parable, David was incensed. He declared that death should come to such a selfish, dishonorable man. Nathan then dropped the bomb of truth: David was that rich man.

In this episode of David's life, we see how a great man with a godly heart cooled his love for the Lord even as his lustful passions heated up. In the aftermath of his sin, David suffered the death of his own child and a home marked by war and bloodshed. Somehow beneath it all, a song sparked in the cold heart of this musical poet. He felt the icy absence of love and cried out for a merciful God to rekindle the fire within him. The repentant king prayed, "Create in me a clean heart, O God, and renew a steadfast spirit within me" (Ps. 51:10).

This is the path back to God. This is the warming of the heart again. Your pain can be replaced with His gain.

DEFINED BY DESTINY

David's life was recreated through repentance. We can experience the same rekindling of our passion for God. He can use our pain as fuel for our future. The Bible tells us that old things will pass away and all things will become new again (2 Cor. 5:17). This is how our tears become life-giving springs. This is new life.

When we hit Pause in the midst of our pain and turn to God, it's the equivalent of putting an ellipsis in the story of our lives. We suspend our usual journey to regain clarification about our direction. Authors Bill Burnett and Dave Evans call this "reframing." In biblical times, changing one's name often expressed this reframing. Jacob, meaning "supplanter" or "trickster," became Israel, or "Prince of God." Abram became Abraham as his destiny was expanded. Saul became the apostle Paul. Barnabas's original name was Joseph.

Jesus followers learn to leverage their pain into a positive history, one that tells a story of pain that has been transformed. This is not revisionist history but a Spirit-fueled metamorphosis. We become new creatures in Christ, and when God looks at our lives, He sees the perfection of His beloved Son (Heb. 11). He reframes our lives into a testimony of faith, a trophy of grace. When you cry out before God, your sharpest pains carve out a pattern of sculptural beauty.

As the Lord changes you and gives your life definition by destiny, you are no longer defined by your pain. You move forward and become known for your courage. You recover from your addiction and help others do the same. You move on from your past conviction and become a servant leader in your community. You no longer put money and status first but instead give generously and advance God's kingdom. You refuse to allow your divorce to deter you from loving again. You express your grief without wallowing in it. You take control of the headline over your life, proclaiming the Lord's goodness in bold, bright colors.

Your new headline doesn't ignore past reality—it redefines it for the future. No matter how unbearable something feels in the moment, we are not only comforted by God's presence but we are also empowered by it. Whatever we face can be redefined. Over the course of my life, I've learned to pivot in painful moments and immediately begin to reframe my circumstance. Instead of focusing on my pain, disappointment, or loss, I try to look for hope, for beauty, for the prophetic words that have hung over my life.

God is for you and can move your ashes into a magnificent story of God's limitless grace. Your pain can define you in positive ways if you allow Him to heal you and use you. We can rest in the power of the Spirit's transcendent love living in us. Paul's declaration assures us that "neither death nor life, nor angels nor principalities nor powers, nor things present nor things to come, nor height nor depth, nor any other created thing, shall be able to separate us from the love of God which is in Christ Jesus our Lord" (Rom. 8:38–39). No matter how painful life becomes, God's perfect love never fails!

YOUR VIEW FROM HERE

No matter how devastating our struggles, disappointments, and troubles are, they are only temporary. No matter what happens to you, no matter the depth of tragedy or pain you face, no matter how death stalks you and your loved ones, the Resurrection promises you a future of immeasurable good.

—JOSH MCDOWELL

YOUR PROPHETIC LIFE MAP

1. What are the three most painful events or seasons of your life so far? How has each one shaped you to be who you are right now? How has God used those times of suffering to draw you closer to Him and His purpose for your life? Are you able to see any good come from what once seemed only bad?

2. Who are the spiritual heroes and mentors in your life right now, the people you know who encourage, inspire, and support you along your journey of faith? How has their past pain been transformed by God? What can you learn from their testimony to His power?

3. Take a deep breath and quiet your heart before God. Invite the Holy Spirit to infuse you with His peace and power. After basking in His presence for a few minutes, reflect on your life and how you presently see God at work. Think about how you would summarize the way the Lord is transforming your life's pain into something glorious for His eternal purposes. Try to come up with a headline, using no more than eight words, that expresses this ongoing process. Thank Him for all that He's doing as you seek your next steps in pursuit of the prophetic life of joy and peace that He has given you. Write out your headline and post it in a prominent spot where you will see it every day.

The Lord is close to the brokenhearted and saves those who are crushed in spirit.
—Psalm 34:18 NIV

CHAPTER 15

THE AMAZING RACE

Persevering as the Winner You Are

> Do you not know that in a race all the runners
> run, but only one gets the prize? Run in such a
> way as to get the prize.
> —1 Corinthians 9:24 NIV

> Be who God meant you to be and you will set the
> world on fire.
> —Saint Catherine of Siena

Your life began with your mother and father. For whatever reason, they were attracted to each other, and you became the fruit of their relationship. Your life began with perfect timing. Seconds counted, challenges arose, but you grew and matured. Embarking on life's difficult journey of hide-and-seek, you developed as a human being created in God's image.

Despite incredible odds stacked against your survival, you came to life in that first moment of conception. The seed that delivered the DNA package that would become you traveled an arduous journey to unite with your mother's egg. Up to one billion other seeds filled with "potential yous" were released, filling less than two teaspoons. Each one of the seeds carried a chromosome package to create a human being at conception. The force of entry into your mother's womb was approximately twenty-eight miles per hour. You literally blasted onto the scene!

At this point, having just entered the womb, these sperm were small, each with a tiny tail visible only under a microscope. These sperm cells carried one-half the chromosomes necessary to trigger who you would become, while the egg contained the other half. The odds were against conception because only one in five sperm travel in the correct direction from the start. Acidic fluids killed most of the seeds, followed by an army of white blood cells coming to conquer those intruders. They eliminated more than 99.9 percent of all sperm cells, leaving only about ten thousand remaining.

At the top of the ovaries, the remaining seeds could go left or right. Typically, only one tube has an egg waiting, reducing the odds of conception by one-half. Consequently, the number of sperm cells drop to about one thousand passing through the narrow fallopian tube to find the waiting egg, with only around two hundred actually making contact with it. These final seeds attempt to drill through the egg's outer core until one succeeds, releasing a reaction that closes off all other intruders. In the process, the winning sperm loses its tail and delivers its contribution to your chromosome package. The fertilized egg then travels to a safe landing spot to receive nourishment and grow.

UP WHERE YOU BELONG

When you were born approximately nine months later, you had already won the most important race of your existence. Out of almost a billion sperm cells, less than 1 percent reached the egg to fertilize it with new life. You beat the odds! You fought your way to the prize, competing against hundreds of millions, and you won. You are here on purpose. God's Word says, "I will praise You, for I am fearfully and wonderfully made; marvelous are Your works, and that my soul knows very well" (Ps. 139:14).

You are alive for a reason. You are who was needed for this place and this time. God designed you, wonderfully and fearfully. It's no coincidence that you're reading this book at this point in your faith journey. You're right where you're supposed to be!

God actually designs everything with a specific purpose or destiny. You are created for something unique and distinct. You fulfill roles and responsibilities that no one else can fill. On nature programs on television we see the symbiotic and symphonic relationship between many species. All living creatures are part of the glory of God's creation. We are all intertwined with one another. When one species is endangered or becomes extinct, then all others suffer. Environmental chaos ensues.

You are a stabilizer for this planet.

You are fashioned for purpose.

You are created for dominion.

There is a domain waiting for you. You may have forgotten who you are and where you are going, or you may be living in the full abundance of your joyful, prophetic life. Regardless of your current coordinates, God will continue leading you home. He will continue alerting you to choices that you should make and new directions you should take. He marks our lives with prophetic billboards from heaven, drawing us ever closer to Him as we venture forward.

God created you in His own image, instilling you with the capacity to create, love, serve, protect, and thrive. He knew what He was doing when you were conceived, and He knows what He's doing with your life at this very moment. God told the prophet Jeremiah, "Before I formed you in the womb I knew you: before you were born I sanctified you: I ordained you a prophet to the nations" (Jer. 1:4–5). There is no doubt about God's intention.

All that Jeremiah was to become had been fashioned by God with unique structure, personality, mental capacity, and soul. His life had already been anointed as one set apart to serve God. Knowing God's impartial love for His children, I'm inclined to believe that God instills the same intentional divine design in you and me. We are structured for certain conditions and environments, traveling by faith on a beautiful journey filled with mysteries, surprises, and discoveries of God's goodness.

O CANADA!

Like the largest, most elaborate puzzle ever created, your life presents a mystery to be solved. God wastes nothing, and all the pieces eventually come together, some sooner and some later. And some won't fit into place until you're with Him in heaven. But if you're willing to walk by faith in the power of God's Spirit, you begin to see evidence of His hand in your life more clearly.

I'm still amazed at the revelation of God's presence at work in my life. For instance, when I was in fifth grade, out teacher introduced a new class project. We would each randomly select a place in the world, research it thoroughly, and present our findings to the class. She then passed a basket around the room with geographic locations written on folded pieces of paper. One by one each classmate selected a paper, opened it up, and announced their global destination.

We all cheered as different classmates announced the cool,

exotic places they would be researching and reporting on—places like Tahiti, Australia, Iceland, and Chile. When it was my turn, I reached in and pulled out a slip revealing New Brunswick, Canada. I had never heard of it. The response from my peers was tepid at best. Little did I know, however, that my selection would hold keys to my future in several sectors of my life.

I studied as much as I could in a pre-internet world, looking through encyclopedias and contacting the provincial capital of tourism for more information. I learned that New Brunswick was a bilingual province of Canada, part of the Maritime Provinces on the East Coast. It was known for some of the highest tides in the world, which translated to industries like shipbuilding, oil refining, and fishing. I gave my presentation, and it eventually went the path of most other elementary projects, in the trash.

Seven years later, I attended a community college. There, my advisor recommended I take a geography class, but unfortunately all of them were already filled except for one. Days later, I found myself in a small class with only four other students studying the nation of Canada! Please understand, I had no desire to study Canada nor had I ever been there; this class simply fulfilled a requirement.

Nevertheless, I studied every place from Vancouver in the west to Newfoundland in the northeast. I learned about their government, culture, provinces, and capitals. While all this information meant little to me personally at the time, God was equipping me. Looking back, I see this class was another piece of a large puzzle gradually coming together throughout my life.

The next year, while in the parking lot of that college, God spoke to me. I knew immediately I would attend a Bible school and prepare for ministry. It kind of made sense because I loved God and the church. And my brother was already a minister by that time.

But this deep calling and my conviction to obey God resulted in changing directions. After some research, I registered for a school in Missouri.

In my second year at Bible college, I was doing what many young men do after the start of the school year: checking out new female students! During my dating reconnaissance, I spotted a beautiful young woman chatting with a friend of mine. My friend introduced me and then left us to get better acquainted. As we chatted, I immediately noticed she had an accent that sounded British to me. When I asked where she was from, she said, "I'm probably from a place you've never heard of before . . . New Brunswick, Canada."

My heart skipped a beat! I spent the next half hour showcasing my vast knowledge of her homeland based on my fifth grade report and college geography class. She was impressed enough to go out with me. We dated for two years and got married!

After marrying, we worked in ministry until God moved us to New Brunswick. Not only did we live there ten years, but two of our children were born there as dual citizens of Canada and the United States. Most likely, I would not have picked this path, but God knew better and prepared me for what was ahead. He had selected my life's path, and it's been better than anything I could have imagined.

Now, after being married to this wonderful woman named Cindy for more than forty years, I look back and marvel at God's cleverness. He cares about each and every detail of our lives, even the ones that seem random, trivial, and mundane to us.

PIECES OF YOUR PUZZLE

When Cindy and I first got married, we used to put jigsaw puzzles together—really big puzzles—with what seemed like thousands of pieces! This was obviously before we had children. We would lay all the pieces out on the kitchen table and work on them for days. When we were done, we would hang the completed puzzles on our walls.

You've probably worked on puzzles like these. They require considerable time and focus as you search for interlocking pieces to become corners and edges. Then, looking at the cover of the box for the finished image, you zoom in on obvious spots with unique colors and shapes in the picture. That cover image is the key to unlocking the puzzle and determining how all the pieces fit together.

I can't think of a better metaphor for discerning prophetic revelations in your life. God gives us different pieces throughout our life. They vary in color and intensity, size and shape. Some are dark and foreboding. Others are bright and fun. Yet they are all needed to make your beautiful life-picture appear.

Sometimes we feel like we're going through life with a puzzle box filled with seemingly random pieces. The dark fragments may reflect minor setbacks and small difficulties in life, such as moving away from friends and changing schools during childhood. Other pieces of life's puzzle may represent more serious issues stemming from greater disappointments, pervasive rejection, or serious levels of abuse. A few pieces may seem entirely black, obscured by the devastating loss of a loved one, a chronic illness, or a debilitating injury.

Among the bright pieces, there are childhood awards and achievements, family vacations, happy times with friends, and milestones like getting a driver's license or graduating. Other colorful pieces may include starting new jobs, traveling to different countries, and experiencing new cultures. Dating and meeting a spouse might shape part of the puzzle, along with starting a family.

We each carry around many pieces of our life's puzzle, but we don't always try to put the pieces together. But each piece reveals a clue about what God is up to and where He wants to take you. Each one signals something about who you are and how He made you. The good, the bad, and the ugly have all made it into your puzzle box. If put together properly, they reveal the masterpiece of the beautiful life God has intended for you.

DON'T MISS YOUR MIRACLE

Over time, you may have realized that all the colors work together for something majestic and fulfilling. You may have also recognized a pattern of self-destructive tendencies along the dark corners. Yet so many pieces merely seem confusing, unclear, and ambiguous. It's so tempting to get stuck just carrying around this assorted box of your life's puzzle pieces.

As we've seen throughout these pages, however, these pieces are anything but random. They are spiritual clues and heavenly bread crumbs, divine mile markers on our journey of faith through life. As followers of Jesus, we know that God holds the box cover for the puzzle of our lives. Throughout life, we have prophetic moments when God shows us the box cover. We call them epiphanies and revelations. They might happen while reading the Bible, watching a movie, or hiking our favorite trail. They occur in conversations with spouses, kids, parents, friends, coworkers, colleagues, and strangers. They emerge in dreams and daydreams, in divine coincidences that are conspicuous in their unveiling.

I've been blessed to see my box cover, over and over again, usually just for a few moments at a time. But each glimpse lasts long enough for me to see a bit more of who I am, what I need to do next, and where God is leading me. I suspect my experience is similar to what Jesus encountered as He moved through several days of great revelation in the inauguration of His ministry. For instance, Jesus' baptism was His box-cover moment. When His cousin John baptized Him, the heavens opened and God spoke and said, "This is My beloved Son, in whom I am well pleased" (Matt. 3:17). Pieces were being added to Jesus' box, and He was getting a major look at the big picture.

Christ was then led into the wilderness to be tempted by the Devil. This experience had the potential to hinder or truncate an otherwise beautiful life. Instead, Jesus set an example for us by resisting the Devil with God's Word and coming out of the wilderness in the power of the Spirit. His dark pieces were shaped into details of empowerment for His journey.

Similarly, Jesus likely experienced the power of revelation as He saw various pieces come together. When He went into the synagogue and stood up to read, Jesus opened the book and looked for a specific passage, which we recognize as the beginning of Isaiah 61. This selection was not random or accidental but revealed the mission and manifesto of the living Christ:

> The Spirit of the LORD is upon Me,
> Because He has anointed Me
> To preach the gospel to the poor;
> He has sent Me to heal the brokenhearted,
> To proclaim liberty to the captives
> And recovery of sight to the blind;
> To set at liberty those who are oppressed;
> To proclaim the acceptable year of the LORD.

Then He closed the book, and gave it back to the attendant and sat down. And the eyes of all who were in the synagogue were fixed on Him.

(LUKE 4:18–20)

Jesus then stunned the crowd by saying, "Today this Scripture is fulfilled in your hearing" (v. 21). He was owning that revelation over His life. Jesus was showing His box cover to everyone, making His identity and purpose clear.

God's Word holds keys to your destiny. You, too, have had box-cover moments with more to come. As you see more and more of your box-image portrait revealed, you will understand more of your purpose and experience more of God's love. As you see and hear more and more of what God thinks about you, your soul will leap and your heart will overflow.

We see this outpouring in Mary, the mother of Jesus, as she responded to the angel's promise of a child. This young woman, no doubt rather ordinary, was suddenly touched by the extraordinary. Her response was a template for what all Christian responses should be in a moment of divine confirmation. "I am the Lord's servant," Mary answered. "May your word to me be fulfilled" (Luke 1:38 NIV). In other words, she was "all in" on the picture of her life she had just seen. She was likely afraid, uncertain, and anxious about surrendering herself so completely, but she didn't want to miss out on the miracle of giving birth to God's Son. Don't miss your miracle!

DIVINE DETECTIVE

The picture gracing the box cover of your life's puzzle is stunning. It's a work of supernatural art that only the Master could have produced through His divine brushstrokes. As this beautiful treasure map of the soul is unfurled, you see more and more clearly. You become attuned to God's voice and synchronized with the rhythm of His steps.

God has crafted you from the beginning to be a champion. The revelation of what He has for you is beyond your imagination.

Regardless of how big it might be, your response should always reflect Mary's: "I'm yours, Lord, show me the way." Or, in modern vernacular, "I'm all in. Sign me up, and let's do it!" Every time you see glimpses of God's purpose for you, affirm with a *yes*.

Take a look at the pieces of your life and continue putting them together. Others may help you, but you are the one that has access to your puzzle. You will be amazed at His attention to detail in preparation for what you were designed to be and do.

Mark Twain famously stated, "The two most important days of your life are the day you are born and the day you find out why." Today might be your day to fit more pieces together and see God's design for your life. God's Word reminds us, "It is the glory of God to conceal a matter, but the glory of kings is to search out a matter" (Prov. 25:2). Be a student of your life, a detective of the divine.

We must pursue God wholeheartedly and live by His Spirit. James urged, "Draw near to God and He will draw near to you" (James 4:8). This has always been the basis for our romance with God: we love because we have first been loved. In Song of Solomon 2, the lover runs through the hills and comes to the beloved's house. This is a traditional picture parable of God's great intentional love for us. He calls for you to come out from behind your wall. You have to respond to His lead. Always dance with the one who brought you to the party. With your life as a celebration of discovery, your partner is always God. Continue searching out ways that God has already been moving in your life.

HUNGER FOR THE HOLY

As we conclude our time together in these pages, I pray you will move forward with confidence in your ongoing pilgrimage of faith. No matter what has happened in the past, no matter what obstacle you encounter in the future, you will always overcome it through the presence of God, the love of Christ, and the power of the Spirit. Throughout your journey, persevere as you learn more about yourself and discover waypoints and thin places where God reveals Himself to you more fully. Heeding the call of Jesus, you will draw closer and closer to Him. As life events unfold, you will find your route modified, recalibrated, detoured, and redirected—often without notice. Nonetheless, you take the next step in faith, and with each one, it is no longer you that lives but Christ living in you.

Whatever you do, you must never give up!

If you're struggling, stuck, or stalled, remain faithful and obedient and wait on the Lord. You may feel so lost, but God is still looking after you and seeking your heart. He created Eden and He wants it back. God longs to walk with you in the cool of the day. Eden is being recovered in you.

Even if you miss some points along the way, take a wrong turn, or have a meltdown, there is one truth that remains: Jesus is the Alpha and Omega, the beginning and the end. Your life began with God crafting you in the womb and will end with you being ushered into His presence.

Don't abandon the hope we have in Christ. Instead, pay attention to your soul's hunger. Spiritual hunger for more will always motivate you forward. Hunger transcends personal culture. A hungry person is not concerned about being embarrassed or even judged. Esau was willing to give away all that was promised to him for one bowl of soup. Hunger can lead you into wrong places, to associate with wrong people, doing the wrong things. No other pursuit will fill the void inside you.

Your future and the assurance of it rest in Jesus Christ. Your hunger for Him will transform you into a radical Christian. Hunger in the New Testament caused the woman with an ostracizing ailment to press through a crowd desperate for one touch of Jesus. She was filled. A blind man yelled out, breaking cultural norms. Being hushed by the disciples, he cried out all the louder. He was filled. The friends of a paralyzed man could not get into the house where Jesus was ministering, so ignoring all limitations, they tore off the roof and lowered their broken friend into the midst of Jesus. He was filled. Hunger caused Roman centurion Cornelius to mimic that religious activity of Jews, resulting in God's seeing his humble faith and using him to open massive spiritual doors. Hunger will make it happen. God is not afraid of your persistence. Don't give up!

Just as bread grows stale over time, we need fresh manna every day of our lives. I can encounter the Lord through all the different ways I've shared with you here, and yet so many distractions attempt to harden my heart. Attitudes, actions, and mentalities start moving in to rob me of the potential open gate into a new level of Christlikeness.

What do I do? How do I keep going? I turn toward Him with my hungry heart. When you turn to the Lord with hunger as a little child, He shows up.

As you venture into your destiny, some things will happen as planned, and others will not have been on your menu. Never despair. Simply trust Him to feed you with goodness and lead you by the hand.

Stay hungry for all that is holy. Always know that if you cultivate closeness with God, He will always be just a lean away. Learn to lean. Move toward the softer space. Choose peace. Love much. Judge little. Celebrate everything. Choose Jesus first, every way, every day. May the life you live become a narrative offered up to God. I leave you with three prayers made by Saint Patrick:

Let me live to complete the dream I have for you God!
Let me live until my season of worship is complete!

Let me live long enough to bear a saving word to those outside of your grace![1]

Live long and prosper, my friend! Godspeed on your prophetic journey!

YOUR VIEW FROM HERE

Perseverance is not a long race; it is many short races one after the other.

—WALTER ELLIOT

1. As you look back at your life, what patterns emerge revealing how God has prepared you for each step along the way? What pieces of your life's puzzle have fallen into place and reveal a glimpse of His ongoing masterpiece?
2. What pieces of your life's puzzle continue to trouble you because they don't seem to fit or make sense? What's required for you to surrender them in faith and continue moving forward? How can you respond like Mary, the mother of Jesus, who fully gave herself to God's plan for her life?
3. After spending a few moments in prayer, look back through the pages of this book. How would you describe your experience reading it? What have you learned? What have you enjoyed the most? How has God communicated through your reading of it? Which chapter continues to resonate with you? Why? What do

you think God wants you to do as you continue moving forward on your prophetic journey of faith?

The God of all grace, who called you to his eternal glory in Christ, after you have suffered a little while, will himself restore you and make you strong, firm and steadfast.

—1 PETER 5:10 NIV

ACKNOWLEDGMENTS

I want to thank my wife, Cindy, and our family for all their thoughts and input and unwavering support for my many ventures. They provide the many lessons and revelations that fill this book. Thanks, Megan, for your energy and insight in preparing for this book launch.

I also want to recognize key influences and friendships that have shaped my thoughts and constructs especially regarding the prophetic and the voice of God:

Bill Johnson, John Arnott, Paul Manwaring, Graham Cooke, Joseph Garlington, Rob McMillan, Marc Dupont, Roger Ames, Chris Witt, and many others.

Special thanks to my publisher and all who were involved: Joel Kneedler, Janene MacIvor, and Dudley Delffs. An easy group to work with, both professional and personal.

I also want to thank the Holy Spirit for continued friendship. You have shown me much and led me well.

NOTES

CHAPTER 1: MAP MAKING

1. Buzz Aldrin, *Guideposts*, https://www.guideposts.org/better-living
/life-advice/finding-life-purpose/guideposts-classics-buzz-aldrin
on-communion-in-space.

CHAPTER 2: YOU ARE HERE

1. Daniel Pink, *Drive* (New York: Penguin Group, 2009), 115.

CHAPTER 3: MAP READING

1. Stephen Covey, *The Seven Habits of Highly Effective People* (New
York: Simon and Shuster, 1989), 98.

CHAPTER 4: TRAILBLAZING

1. "'Queen of the curve' Zaha Hadid Dies Aged 65 from Heart
Attack," *The Guardian*, November 29, 2016, retrieved March 12,
2019, https://www.theguardian.com/artandsdesign/2016/mar/31
/star-architect-zaha-hadid-dies-aged-65.
2. John O'Donohue, Eternal Echoes (New York: Cliff Street Books
/Harper Collins, 1999), xxv.

CHAPTER 5: NOT TO SCALE

1. Rabbi Daniel Lapin, *Thou Shall Prosper* (Hoboken, New Jersey: John Wiley and Sons, 2010), 1.
2. Brian Zahnd, *Beauty Will Save the World* (Lake Mary, Florida: Charisma House, 2012), xiii.

CHAPTER 8: BORDERS AND BOUNDARIES

1. Steve Witt, *Voices: Understanding and Responding to the Language of Heaven* (Shippensburg, PA: Destiny Image, 2007), 141. Used by permission of Destiny Image.
2. Jim Collins, *Good to Great* (New York: HarperCollins, 2001), 179.

CHAPTER 9: NATURAL WONDERS

1. Michael Mitton, *Restoring the Woven Cord* (Abingdon, UK: The Bible Reading Fellowship, 1995), 65.

CHAPTER 11: TOUR GUIDE

1. Bob Mumford, *Take Another Look at Guidance* (Plainfield, NJ: Logos Publishing, 1971), 65.]
2. Richard Florida, *Who's Your City?* (New York: Basic Books, 2008), 159.
3. Phyllis Korkki, "Job Satisfaction vs. a Big Paycheck," *The New York Times*, Sept. 11, 2010, https://www.nytimes.com/2010/09/12/jobs/12search.html.
4. John O'Donohue, *Anam Cara: The Book of Celtic Wisdom* (New York: Cliff Street Books/HarperCollins, 1997), xviii.
5. Ed Silvoso, Anointed for Business (Ventura, California: Regal Books, 2002), 28.

CHAPTER 13: LONGITUDE AND LATITUDE

1. Bill Bennett and Dave Evans, *Designing Your Life* (New York: Knopf, 2016), 145.

NOTES

CHAPTER 14: UNEXPECTED TURBULENCE

1. Dale Carnegie, *How to Stop Worrying and Start Living* (New York: Simon & Schuster), 138.
2. Andy Andrews, *The Seven Decisions* (Nashville: Thomas Nelson, 2008), 99.

CHAPTER 15: THE AMAZING RACE

1. Calvin Miller, *The Path of Celtic Prayer* (Downers Grove, Illinois: Intervarsity Press, 2007), 123.

ABOUT THE AUTHOR

Steve Witt is the senior leader of Bethel Cleveland. His passion to see believers come into their God-given potential has motivated him to plant churches in the United States and Canada. He's a strategic builder with a prophetic gift. His life has been marked by timely prophetic encounters and dreams that have guided his life and given direction and encouragement to many. Steve is the author of *Voices* and the developer of training material for churches and individuals. Steve has served on numerous boards, including the Partners in Harvest Apostolic team based in Toronto, Canada, and the Vineyard Canada Leadership team. Steve partners in ministry with his wife, Cindy. He has four adult children and four grandchildren. In his free time he enjoys reading, writing, and travelling, especially to Italy. His mission in life is the continued advancement of people on their journeys in God.

Steve Witt

E-Course: *Your Prophetic Life Map*
- An indepth course on discovering your God-Crafted Destiny based on the book

Live Map Training with Steve Witt or associates at your church or business

Online Mentorship available to pastors and emerging leaders
- Key steps to becoming fruitful in your calling

The Devoted Emerging Prophetic Community
- A worldwide community pursuing a path of revelatory leadership

---

Visit us now to enroll
Bring your future into your present
Let's map this life together

www.stevewitt.com

For Full-Size Charts
Visit
ThomasNelson.com/p/YourPropheticLifeMap/